TEXTXET

Studies in comparative literature 2

Series Editors
C.C. Barfoot and Theo D'haen

The Phaedra Syndrome
Of Shame and Guilt in Drama

Albert S. Gérard

Rodopi
Amsterdam - Atlanta, GA
1993

CIP-GEGEVENS KONINKLIJKE BIBLIOTHEEK, DEN HAAG

Gérard, Albert S.

The Phaedra Syndrome
Of Shame and Guilt in Drama
Albert S. Gérard. - Amsterdam - Atlanta, GA 1993: Rodopi.
(Textxet, ISSN 0927-5754 ; no. 2)
Met lit. opg., reg.
ISBN: 90-5183-489-6
Trefw.: schuldgevoelens in het toneel / schaamtegevoelens in het toneel.

Cover design: Hendrik van Delft

© Editions Rodopi B.V., Amsterdam - Atlanta, GA 1993
Printed in The Netherlands

Books by Albert S. Gérard

L'Idée romantique de la poésie en Angleterre
Paris, Les Belles Lettres, 1955

English Romantic Poetry
Berkeley, University of California Press, 1968

Les Tambours du néant: Le problème existentiel dans le roman américain
Brussels, La Renaissance du Livre, 1969

Four African Literatures
Berkeley, University of California Press, 1971

Etudes de littérature africaine francophone
Dakar, Nouvelles Editions Africaines, 1977

African-Language Literatures
Washington, Three Continents Press & London, Longman, 1981

Comparative Literature and African Literatures
Pretoria, Via Afrika, 1983

Essais d'histoire littéraire africaine
Sherbrooke (Canada), Naaman, 1984

Contexts of African Literature
Amsterdam/Atlanta, Rodopi, 1990

Littératures en langues africaines
Paris, Mentha, 1992

Baroque Tragedy: Essays on Seventeenth-Century Western Drama
Liège: L3—Liège Language and Literature (forthcoming)

Editor: *European-Language Writing in Sub-Saharan Africa*
Budapest, Akadémiai Kiadó, 1986

CONTENTS

Introduction 1

1 The Honour Code Questioned: Euripides' *Hippolutos* (428 BC). 5
2 Reason and Guilt: Seneca's *Phaedra* (First Century AD) 20
3 The Ethics of Fear: Bandello's *Novella 44* (1554) · · · 38
4 Justice and Revenge Reconciled: Lope de Vega's *El castigo sin venganza* (1634) 48
5 The Triumph of Guilt: Racine's *Phèdre* (1677) · · · · 72
6 *Phèdre*, Racine and the Anguish of the Times · · · · 107

Conclusion 123

Bibliography 136

INTRODUCTION

In one of his posthumous works Edward Gibbon recounts the following events, which took place in Ferrara in 1425:

> Under the reign of Nicholas III, Ferrara was polluted with a domestic tragedy. By the testimony of a maid, and his own observation, the Marquis of Este discovered the incestuous loves of his wife Parisina, and Hugo his bastard son, a beautiful and valiant youth. They were beheaded in the castle, by the sentence of a father and husband, who published his shame, and survived their execution. He was unfortunate, if they were guilty: if they were innocent, he was still more unfortunate: nor is there any possible situation in which I can sincerely approve the last act of justice of a parent (701).

Byron's poem "Parisina" was inspired by this passage. But the sorry tale of Ugo d'Este had first been given literary shape in the sixteenth century by Matteo Bandello. One of the many Italian story-tellers who were immensely popular during the Renaissance and became purveyors of source material for such as Shakespeare or Lope de Vega, Bandello is better known in England for the original script of *Romeo and Juliet*. In his own day, however, this Dominican friar was widely esteemed as a first-rate conversationalist. He had a special flair for stories that were cleverly cast in moral guise while catering for the prurient tastes and sadistic proclivities of the most refined audiences. The story of Ugo d'Este first reached print in Lucca in 1544 as *Novella 44* in the first volume of Bandello's *Novelliere* (I, 514-24): it had taken little more than a century for the juicy tale with its attractive gory ending to be raised from the lowly sphere of gossip to the durable status of written recording. After another century it was promoted to a higher level of literary accomplishment when Lope de Vega adapted it for the stage as *El castigo sin venganza* (1631). If the Spanish playwright chose to turn this anecdote into one of his most memorable (and controversial) plays, it may be worth our while to speculate what kind of potential significance he can have found in it.

Bandello's narrative illustrates an archetypal situation of transgression which is endowed with peculiar relevance whenever the structure of society (as frequently happens) encourages elderly gentlemen to marry attractive teenage girls, even though they may already be provided with teenage sons of their own. In the nutshell of the nuclear family the emergence of a sexual relationship between the husband's son and his stepmother offers a fascinating diversity of subversive trends, especially where the "natural" phallocratic authority of the *pater familias* is sanctioned by public opinion and religious dogma. Such a situation compounds adultery with incest. It brings into play the fundamental psychological motivations of love and honour, sex and vengeance. It exemplifies the utter disruption of natural order and moral hierarchies. It almost inevitably compels author and reader alike to pass moral judgment and to take sides in the contest between natural impulses and ethical precepts, as we have just seen even a historian like Gibbon doing, with his inimitably British sense of balance and fair play.

The world-wise Bandello was more artfully restrained. He did not fail to note that Niccoló, "il piú feminil uomo che a quei tempi si ritrovasse", neglected his lusty young wife, so that sexual frustration and conjugal humiliation appear as extenuating circumstances for Parisina when she sets out to seduce her stepson. Through skilful use of the mighty weapons at the disposal of her sex she succeeds in this undertaking, and Bandello dryly observes "che se Fedra cosí bella e leggiadra fosse stata, io porto ferma credenza che averebbe a suoi piaceri il suo amato Ippolito reso pieghevole". This remark reveals the writer's awareness that he is dealing with a variant of a basic pattern also illustrated in the Phaedra-Hippolytus-Theseus triangle: the destruction of order, moral and social, that occurs when the primal figure of authority, the father-husband (whose functional significance is re-inforced by the fact that he is also head of the state) sees his power challenged and his honour threatened by those who are most closely bound to obey and respect him: his son and his wife. The woman's enslavement to sexual urges initiates the criminal process that violates the social institution of marriage, the moral prohibition of incest, God's sacred commands and, most objectionable perhaps, the taboo against sexual competition between different generations which is the very foundation of family hierarchy. This is what I venture to call "the Phaedra syndrome".

Introduction

In earlier centuries a medieval Bandello might have referred to the Bible: the Joseph story in Genesis 39 likewise relates how a virtuous young man is subjected to illicit sollicitations from a more experienced woman, whose husband happens to be his lord, protector and owner. Like the classical Hippolytus, the biblical Joseph resists the temptress's allurements and is duly rewarded when the irate woman falsely accuses him of attempting to rape her. Comparatists have not been blind to the similarity, but their attention has usually focussed on the disdained woman's revenge. To the modern reader this is of course the most conspicuously dramatic element in either story.[1]

Writing in the middle of the sixteenth century, Bandello presumably found it more effective to display his humanistic erudition: Seneca's tragedies had been printed in Ferrara in the early 1480s; during the first half of the next century there were further editions (including the Aldine edition in 1517), translations, Italian versions and performances.[2] Bandello could legitimately expect his cultured audience to be familiar with Latin works that had been virtually forgotten during the Middle Ages, and we can understand that he selected Seneca rather than the Bible for a comparison with the tragic fate of Ugo d'Este and Parisina.

The basic pattern is the universal triangle involving a middle-aged husband, his lustful young wife and his attractive young son. Throughout literary history it has provided subject matter for many genres, from high tragedy through comedy, down to vaudeville. The particular sub-pattern illustrated in the Joseph and Hippolytus tales is characterized by the fact that the husband has a high status in society and deserves more than the usual share of respect because he is father, or a father substitute, to the young man. In all likelihood it originated in the unfathomable recesses of international oral lore. Like many folktales, both the biblical and classical episodes were meant to convey an ethical message. They are typical test stories, cautionary tales whose educational function is to warn the young males of the tribe against coveting or yielding to, the seductive wives of their elders and betters.

---

[1] The motif of the woman as temptress and accuser is discussed in comparative terms by Elisabeth Frenzel in *Motive der Weltliteratur*, 160-70. For its application to the Phaedra story, see Paul Bénichou's brilliant essay, "Hippolyte requis d'amour et calomnié", 237-323.

[2] For a general survey of Seneca's influence, see *Der Einfluss Senecas auf das europäische Drama*, ed. Eckard Lefèvre.

The danger is demonstrated through four structural stages: the young man's virtue is first established; next comes the temptation and rejection scene; this is followed by the woman's vengeful response; the climax is the young man's undeserved punishment. Two points are of central interest in this hypothetical original pattern: the positive hero is the chaste, law-abiding young man, who demonstrates his ability to control the most impetuous of all natural impulses when it violates the norms of approved behaviour; the woman is described as a vessel of iniquity, a prey to basic urges and, if thwarted, a vengeful, slanderous creature.

In the course of written literature a shift in focus occurred, which is illustrated by the titles given to the written works that deal with the Theseus-Hippolytus-Phaedra story. The two plays of Euripides are known as *Hippolutos kaluptomenos* (now lost) and *Hippolutos stephanêphoros*; Seneca's version is known either as *Hippolytus* or *Phaedra*; Renaissance and seventeenth-century plays are titled *Hippolytus*, *Phaedra* or *Hippolytus and Phaedra*, but Racine, after some hesitation, decided in favor of *Phèdre*, as did Swinburne in his dramatic poem of 1866 and Gabriele d'Annunzio for his play of 1906. There must be some reason for this. It may be tentatively suggested that, to writers concerned with moral issues, psychological problems and dramatic momentum, the female protagonist is intrinsically more fascinating. The immaculate fortitude of a young man who is presented as a model of virtue, who knows how he is expected to behave and unquestioningly strives and manages to comply, is of slight intellectual or dramatic interest. The female temptress is potentially a far more engrossing figure. Unless she be a mindless nymphomaniac, she must be aware of the contradiction between duty and her desire; she must realize that, in initiating the transgressive process, she is courting danger in a variety of ways: physical punishment, social disapproval and/or (in a Christian context) eternal damnation. As a free agent, she has to make a fateful choice, and this choice must needs be motivated.

The purpose of this essay is to discuss the ways that several important writers in the course of many centuries have handled this character, how they analysed its motivations, in what light they presented its emotions and actions. It is also, in a humbly tentative way, to venture a few suggestions as to the relationship between their treatment of the Phaedra figure and the moral and intellectual climate of their times.

1

THE HONOUR CODE QUESTIONED: EURIPIDES' *HIPPOLUTOS* (428 BC)

A number of distinguished Hellenists have strenuously attempted to reconstruct Euripides' first *Hippolutos* from what scant remnants have survived in a variety of sources; their purpose has usually been to trace the genesis of Seneca's Latin play on the subject.[1] It would be a waste of time to base any serious discussion on such conjectural texts. Yet, from a caustic hint in Aristophanes' *The Frogs*, it has been inferred that this was indeed a Hippolytus-centred play, in which Phaidra sets out to seduce her stepson in as crudely direct a way as does the wife of Potiphar in Genesis. The playwright is usually supposed to have recast the play because the Athenian audience objected to having the wife of Theseus, the founder of Athens, portrayed as a kind of whore. If there is any truth in this hypothesis, it is significant that the recasting took the shape of a sophisticated working out of the Queen's psychology. *Hippolutos stephanêphoros* testifies to an incipient shift of the emphasis from Hippolutos to Phaidra, confirming Bénichou's suggestion — that "sitôt entrée dans la littérature, la fable a tendu à glisser du héros vers l'héroïne" (255): the traditional cautionary tale becomes a vehicle for the analysis of tangled issues, in which is it possible to find a reflection of the ideals and taboos of successive ages. The moral conflict in the Queen's mind sets the tone for the whole play. Indeed, competent scholars from Kitto (215) to Grene (159) are of the opinion that the second half of the play, after her suicide, is distinctly weaker in dramatic interest and stylistic quality. This in turn raises the possibility that Euripides, in reworking his subject-matter, had become sensitive to one aspect of the situation which he, like the author of Genesis, had first chosen to overlook: the second Phaidra is not swayed

---

[1] This is one of the main preoccupations of Zintzen, Dingel and Paratore.

unreflectingly by unbridled lust; instead, she is eloquently tormented by her consciousness of the antinomy between sexual gratification and her moral duty as a wife and stepmother. What matters for our present purpose is the nature of this conflict and of the values at stake.

It has long been recognized that the moral check which prevents Phaidra from seeking immediate sexual fulfilment is her concern with *eukleia*, which Hans Strohm correctly isolated as "das wichtigste Leitmotiv des Dramas" (104). The word is usually translated, not very felicitously, as "fame", "reputation", "honour", or even "glory". It is derived from *kleos* (rumour) and refers to public opinion's favourable appraisal of a person's conduct. Phaidra's overriding preoccupation is, literally, to be "well spoken of".

In present-day cultured circles such regard for other people's valuation is professedly held in low esteem. It is nevertheless one of the earliest and most enduring principles of ethical assessment developed by human societies: it is the very foundation of what anthropologists call "shame cultures", those whose members, in George F. Jones's conveniently terse definition, "avoid evil deeds mainly to escape public disgrace or disapproval [and] perform good ones mainly to gain public honor" (13). Margaret Mead has described this as a "mechanism by which desired behavior is induced and undesired behavior prevented" (493). There is nothing primitive about it. Few members of the Renaissance aristocracy would have disputed Iago's assertion that "Good name in man and woman .../ Is the immediate jewel of their souls" (*Othello*, III, iii, 155-56). Contemporary history provides notorious examples of consequential deeds performed by illustrious persons not on account of their inherent usefulness, but for the sake of the way they will be "perceived" by the voters. Throughout the history, literary and otherwise, of the Western world, the need for public esteem and the concomitant fear of public disapproval have been a central motive for purposeful action. The search for *la gloire* is a major theme in Corneille. In his *Arte nuevo de hacer comedias*, Lope de Vega had proclaimed that

> Los casos de la honra son mejores,
> porque mueven con fuerza a toda gente,

a piece of advice that was dutifully followed by most Spanish playwrights of the *siglo de oro*. But even in the Middle Ages, when

Christianity was supposed to reign supreme, Cassio's notion that "reputation" is "the immortal part" of one's self, so that death is better than shame or dishonour, was the object of such a wide consensus in the epic poetry of the Western world, that it must have been more than a literary commonplace: from *Beowulf* to the *Hildebrandslied* and the *Chanson de Roland*, it is constantly presented as a vital force in the actual experience of the warrior class in Europe's feudal and pre-feudal society. As to ancient Greece, E.R. Dodds noted as early as 1951 that "the strongest moral force which Homeric man knows is not the fear of god, but respect for public opinion" (18). The Greek word for this concern for social approval is *aidôs*, a concept which was heavily loaded with positive connotations until the fifth century BC, as was convincingly demonstrated by Carl Eduard von Erffa. It denotes a person's quasi religious reverence for conformity with the expectations of society in his/her relationships with lineage and family, social superiors, and also social inferiors seeking favours: *eukleia*, a good reputation, is the supreme reward for scrupulous observance of the requirements of *aidôs*; conversely, evil repute, *duskleia*, is the ultimate punishment inflicted on those who violate the demands of *aidôs*; it is to be avoided at all costs, even at the cost of life.

Phaidra, therefore, describes a genuinely deadly dilemma when she informs the Nurse that since her (as yet unspoken) love is a "criminal madness" (248), it is better that she should die rather than suffer it to be disclosed. According to the traditional honour code, this is the correct course of action even though Phaedra knows that she is not responsible for her illicit passion, a curse (*atê*) thrown upon her by Aphrodite: in a shame culture, the notion that there can be no culpability without responsibility does not obtain. The rationale underlying her dilemma is made clear when she traces her inner evolution after she had fallen in love with her stepson (392-400): from the first, she had decided to keep silent and conceal her feelings; next, she endeavoured to eradicate this dangerous passion; as this proved impossible, she realized that the only way out was to die. As she now ponders (317-31), self-inflicted death will ensure that the "stain in her heart" will stay there, that all will remain ignorant of her hidden sin, and that out of her shameful inclination she will win good, and so preserve public esteem.

Phaidra's first step on the fateful path that leads to her complete ruin occurs when the anguished Nurse formulates her request in the suppliant attitude that ritualistically precludes refusal (335). The code compels the Queen to yield to the old woman's loving entreaties and to disclose "that which should not be heard". The phrase is spoken by the Chorus (362), which goes on to announce that Phaidra is already doomed since she has unveiled the evil in her. What Euripides himself brings to light in this seminal peripeteia is an inner contradiction in the very code by which Phaidra is determined to abide. It is presumably in order to avoid any misunderstanding that he makes her at this point confusedly conscious of this contradiction and of the quandary she is in as a result. Such is the import of the first part of the rhesis usually known as Phaidra's "great speech":

> Many a time in night's long empty space I have pondered on the causes of life's shipwreck. I think that our acts are worse than the quality of our judgment would warrant. There are many who know virtue. We know the good, we apprehend it clearly. But we can't bring it to achievement. Some are betrayed by their own laziness, and others value some other pleasure above virtue. There are many pleasures in life – long gossiping talks, and leisure, that sweet curse. Then there is shame that thwarts us. Shame is of two kinds. The one is harmless, but the other a plague. For clarity's sake, we should not talk of "shame", a single word for two quite different things (375-80).[2]

These last few lines have spawned an inordinate amount of interpretive commentaries designed to clarify how *aidôs*, described as "a pleasure", can be both "harmless" and "a plague on a house".[3] A comparative approach may perhaps help dissipate some of the confusion by briefly examining the complexity of Greek *aidôs* in the light of the semantic fate of a related concept, the shame/honour cluster, in the literatures of Western societies.

---

[2] Quotations are based on David Grene's fine translation, sometimes altered to ensure more literal conformity with the Greek original.

[3] E.R. Dodds' learned article of 1925 was among the first to direct attention to this perplexing passage. For recent discussions, see the essays by Willink (1968), Segal (1970), Solmsen (1973), Manuwald (1979), Kovacs (1980) and Kawashima (1986).

In his study of *Honor in German Literature* George Fenwick Jones called attention to the gradual development of the concept, noting that the "modern meaning of the word *Ehre*, particularly in the sense of personal integrity or inner voice, did not become widespread before the middle of the eighteenth century. In any case, throughout the Middle Ages, the word *êre* usually designated the recognition, respect, reverence or reputation, which a person enjoyed among men, or else physical tokens thereof" (5-6). Spanish *siglo de oro* writers were already acutely aware of potential contradictions: Antonio de Torquemada, in his *Colóquios satíricos*, denounced the antinomy between Christian honour as inner virtue and secular honour as reputation; they are "irreconcilable", he claimed, because the latter "is a vain and proud presumption, and ... all those who desire and strive for honor follow a road which is not the road of the Christian".[4] Much of the Spanish *comedia* focuses on the problems, ethical, social and political, raised by the use of the same word for entirely different notions. In eighteenth-century France, Montesquieu caustically observed that the principle of monarchy "se corrompt encore plus lorsque l'honneur a été mis en contradiction avec les honneurs et que l'on peut être à la fois couvert d'infamies et de dignités" (II, 254).[5] More recently, a British anthropologist of note, Julian Pitt-Rivers, discussing some Mediterranean societies, called attention to the confusion in shame cultures between "honour which derives from virtuous conduct and that honour which situates an individual socially and determines his right to precedence"; he most unexpectedly echoed Phaidra's perplexity when he went on to observe:

> The two senses appear to be so far removed from one another that one may ask why they were, and still are, expressed by the same word, why the languages of Europe are so determined to avoid clarity in this matter (36).

This latter question is certainly relevant to Euripides' use of *aidôs*. In fact, Phaidra's speech signals a dawning awareness that *aidôs* can induce to morally antinomic forms of behaviour. It can lead a person to

---

[4] Quoted by Otis Green, (I, 17), who notes that the contradiction had already been set forth in 1948 by A. García Valdecasas.

[5] One of the most lucid exposition of the duality of "honour" is still that offered in 1958 by Correa in connection with Spanish Golden Age Drama.

act in genuine compliance with the group's expectations and accepted social norms. It can also prompt a person to dissimulation and hypocritical pretence in order to gain or keep public esteem, however undeserved: this is bad *aidôs*. Phaidra is conscious that *aidôs* is of two kinds and that she is not sure how to distinguish between them: this is the root of her tragic predicament.

As Phaidra further rationalizes her death-wish, her train of thought drives her to disclose, somewhat naively and no doubt unwittingly, the inner confusion brought about by her overriding concern for her reputation. The optic imagery is revealing: she confesses that while she does not want her good deeds to remain hidden, neither does she want her shameful deeds to have many witnesses (403-404). That she should curse adulterous wives and the cynicism of those who condone their wickedness (407-12) is logical. But in view of what she has just said about concealing her own wrong-doings, there is an element of equivocation in her vociferous hatred of those who pay lip-service to virtue while privately indulging in lecherous deeds (413-14); most significantly, she adds that what they should fear is exposure (416-18). It is this fear of exposure, she admits, that prompts her to self-destruction: she cannot bear that she should be "discovered" to have brought shame to her husband and children (419-23).

The concluding lines of the rhesis once more bring out the two main points of the whole argument: the only lasting thing in life, for whoever can attain it, is "a clear conscience" (426-27); the Greek phrase, *gnômèn dikaian kagathèn*, refers to the content of the mind, not just conscious thoughts, but also feelings and desires. Phaidra's sinful passion has put this out of her reach. Since Time, as occasion falls, exposes the wicked, she must die because she is determined *not to be seen* as one of them (428-30).

The potential consequences of the code's ambivalence begin to emerge when the Nurse cheerfully comes back announcing that she has had "wiser second thoughts" (436). As far as Phaidra is concerned this initiates a new phase in the action of the play. The modern reader may find it strange that the Queen, despite her concern with reputation, allowed herself, however reluctantly, to be forced into confessing her passion to the Nurse. It is not enough to argue that the introduction of a *confidante* capable of taking temporary control of the situation was necessary for Euripides' dramatic purpose. Hellenic scholars know that Phaidra merely complied with one of the demands of *aidôs* regarding her relationship to social inferiors.[6] Furthermore, it should be remembered that fifth-century Athens was by no means a democracy in the modern, one-man-one-vote sense of the word. Nor of course was the mythic society in which the action is supposed to take place: as Phaidra makes clear (409-11), the code applies only to the "noble houses", the upper classes of society. The Nurse does not belong to her peer group, the social layer that matters. As a member of the lower class, her knowledge and appraisal are irrelevant and immaterial in the Queen's view. The fact remains, however, that when she let the older woman into her secret, she opened the way for outside intervention, albeit in the form of well-meant advice, and eventually for further dissemination of her hidden sin: the Nurse has not heard the arguments in her mistress's "great speech", and once she is back on-stage, she actually offers what might be described as an alternative ethical system. Given her importance in the ensuing stage of the dramatic action, the philosophy underlying her discourse and behaviour deserves careful scrutiny.

In her loving concern for the Queen that good woman's main purpose is to prevent her mistress's death, to ensure her happiness and to preserve her reputation as far as will be feasible, even if this involves, as will soon appear, concealment, dissimulation and criminal dishonesty. For Phaidra, the logic of *aidôs* leads to death so as to avoid exposure. In the Nurse's hierarchy of values life comes uppermost, closely followed by happiness, with reputation, whether deserved or not, far behind. Her basic principle in the conduct of life is the principle of moderation (*mêden agan*, 265), compromise, common sense, which her experience has taught her to value above anything else (251-66): she had already called on this principle when she advised the Queen to overcome her excess of passion. Now that the fateful dilemma is obviously not to be evaded, she argues differently, but still with the same goal in view. Her own rhesis is a counterpart to Phaidra's great speech. In a masterpiece of sophistry she enlists the considerable resources of her rhetoric in the service of the Queen's life and love, skilfully exploiting (in Turato's phrase) "la seduzzione della parola" to give greater efficacy to what Jacqueline de Romilly called "l'excuse de l'invincible amour".

---

[6] On this point, see the observations of Gould and Taplin.

Phaidra's plight, she notes, is by no means exceptional (435). Aphrodite is not withstandable (443), for sex is the very fountainhead of life (446-50) and even the gods are subjected to her power (451-58): how can Phaidra hope to eschew her yoke? (459-65). Addressing the sensitive problem of Phaidra's reputation, she shrewdly argues that many wise husbands have turned a blind eye to their wives' faithlessness or helped their children subdued by the goddess (462-65); it is proper to wise men (and this, presumably, would include Theseus) to ignore what is improper (465-66). Furthermore, it is not suitable for mortals like Phaidra to decide on their own lives (467), for this would be to claim power superior to the gods', thus committing the dread crime of hubris (474-75). She concludes her sermon with temptingly encouraging words: the Queen must bear up being in love; this is a sickness willed by some god; she must turn it into health again; some remedy shall be found: magic incantations, soothing words, and the ingenious devices that women are apt to think out (476-81).

Euripides makes it clear that two opposite systems of valuation are here facing each other. The Chorus: "she speaks more usefully for your present misfortune, but it is you I praise" (482-83). Phaidra: "These are the too fine words that bring ruin to cities and families" (486-87), "never speak such shameful words again" (499). The Nurse: "Shameful, yes, but they are more to the point than your beautiful words" (500). Phaidra and the Nurse impersonate the antinomic aspects of *aidôs*. The compelling moral sense of the Queen is opposed to the pragmatic realism of the older woman. In her advice the latter takes advantage of the loophole inherent in a declining shame culture. To quote Margaret Mead again, "in societies in which the individual is controlled by fear of being shamed, he is safe if no one knows of his misdeeds; he can dismiss his behavior from his mind" (494). The Nurse does not disparage the Queen's scale of values. Ideally, she agrees, Phaidra should not have gone astray by falling in love with her stepson; since she has, she must fall back on "the next best thing" (507-508), that is, follow her advice. Faced with such loving single-mindedness the Queen is in a weak position, since her moral idealism is undermined by her hankering after Hippolutos. It is therefore not surprising that her determination to die breaks down when the Nurse soothingly asserts; "I will arrange all well" (521).

The Queen's passiveness duplicates the pattern which had enabled the Nurse to discover the loved one's name (351). Phaidra refrains from explicitly yielding to the woman's entreaties. Throughout the tense dialogue "good" *aidôs* remains in technical control, as will later be confirmed by omniscient Artemis when she assures Theseus that Phaidra's "frenzied passion" did not detract from her "nobility", since it was "against her will" that she fell "by the Nurse's stratagem" (1300-305). Nevertheless, by the end of the sequence the Nurse feels she can safely conclude that she has received permission to take charge (521). As a result the play changes course and actual action begins to take place. We should not overlook the implications of the fact that the scheme which henceforth governs the development of the story is conceived by a character belonging to the lower classes: the woman's attachment to life above honour and the law, her condoning adultery and even incest (although this latter consideration, curiously, hardly seems to affect Phaidra), her willingness to resort to devious, deceitful procedures in order to achieve her illegitimate ends, all reflect, on the moral plane, her "ignoble" social status.

Hippolutos' indignant refusal ruins her hopes. It also destroys her credibility altogether as she points out with bitter irony: "Had I succeeded, I had been a wise one" (700). Her failure unmasks the inadequacy of her crafty rhetoric, of her world view and of her scale of values. Her show of moderation, worldly wisdom, down-to-earth realism, middle-of-the-road pragmatism, is now exposed as mere wishful thinking rooted in abysmal ineptitude in assessing the Prince's devotion to Artemis.

Now that the Nurse has leaked Phaidra's secret, an entirely new situation is created. The Queen had resolved to die rather than reveal, let alone gratify, her unlawful passion; but the Nurse is no longer the only one in the know: Hippolutos too is informed. Therefore, Phaidra must not simply die: she must die as soon as possible (599).

As the Prince and the Nurse come back on stage Phaidra retires into the palace. It is likely, as Grene surmises, (188) that she overhears the dialogue for, when she reappears, a new thought has obviously impressed itself upon her anguished mind. She has heard the incensed young man proclaim that he cannot keep silent after such revelation (604), that such horrible things should be widely divulged (610), and that his heart remains unpledged to his tongue's oath of secrecy (612). Phaidra has every reason to believe that Hippolutos in his righteous indignation will inform his father of the Nurse's message and spread the news of the Queen's shame throughout the land (690-92). That this must be regarded as her sincere reasoning will be duly confirmed when Artemis explains, to the benefit of Theseus, that his late wife, "fearing lest she be proved a sinner, wrote a letter full of lies" (1310-11). There is indeed uncontrovertible logic in the Queen's inference that she needs to devise a new scheme to protect her reputation (688): before she dies, she must find some way of silencing the young man, or, at any rate — and this is of decisive importance — of ensuring that whatever he may say will not meet credence. While this is the main purpose of the fatal note, her aim, as she herself explains, is also to take vengeance upon Hippolutos' contempt for her feelings. Furthermore, by casting doubt upon his own truthfulness, she will make him share in her anxiety about good repute, and so teach him moderation (728-31).

Keeping in mind that Phaidra cannot possibly realize that her new scheme will lead to Hippolutos' own death in fulfilment of Aphrodite's plan (see 42 ff.), we must ask ourselves what kind of light this fatal decision throws upon her character and upon the significance of her fate. The problem is closely connected to that of ascertaining Euripides' intention in his reshaping of the Phaidra figure. I find it difficult to agree with André Rivier's somewhat perverse interpretation when he expresses doubt "que l'honneur de Phèdre soit desservi par la décision qu'elle prend et par les conséquences de cette décision" and "qu'un Athénien ait vu, dans la mort d'Hippolyte, une issue ternissant l'honneur de Phèdre". David Kovacs, too, asserts that "the bare fact that she causes the death of the young man she thinks is her enemy and the enemy of her good name would not in the fifth century have been regarded, without further encouragement from the poet, as evidence of moral failure". Actually, what is in question at this point is not the death of Hippolutos, but the writing of the slanderous letter, the lethal outcome of which she neither premeditates nor foresees. As Hazel F. Barnes rightly argues, "her greatest crime ... is neither her love nor her suicide but her false accusation of Hippolytus" (89). The mere fact that she resorts to calumny and the smearing of her stepson's deserved reputation for honesty in order to preserve her no longer deserved reputation for faithfulness provides glaring evidence that the Queen has now joined the Nurse in the latter's allegiance to "bad" *aidôs*. The damning similarity is underlined ironically through Phaidra's complacent assertion, as she drives the Nurse away, that "I will manage my own business well" (709): these words, possibly spoken with a touch of sarcasm, echo the older woman's smug assessment of her own intentions in line 521. The irony is double-barrelled, the Queen bitterly parodying her servant, the playwright anticipating the tragic similarity and convergence in the consequences of both women's ill-advised endeavours.

That Phaidra stoops so low as intentionally to smear Hippolutos' good repute with a slanderous lie should be viewed as the nadir in her moral disintegration. Yet the idea of taking revenge upon his contemptuous rejection seems to be only a belated after-thought. The real, wider purpose of the self-inflicted death that will guarantee her truthfulness was fully conveyed at the end of her brief exchange with the Chorus after the Nurse had been finally dismissed. On her request the "noble daughters of Troezen" have sworn by Artemis to wrap in silence all they have heard. In a few terse lines Phaidra then sums up the benefits that she thinks will accrue from her death. This, her only solution, will enable her to transmit an unsullied name to her children; she will not defile the honour of her Cretan lineage; she will not have to beg forgiveness from her husband for being faithless and thus injuring his honour (715-21). Significantly, this corresponds closely to the central feature of the honour code as still observed today in shame-culture societes. Honour is not just a personal matter: it is a group concept. The dishonour incurred by any individual reflects on the whole lineage. In shame-culture societies, as Pitt-Rivers observes, while "the greatest dishonour of a man derives from the impurity of his wife," "honour is an hereditary quality" and "the shame of the mother is transmitted to the children" (31).

In *The Greeks and the Irrational* E.R. Dodds, who pioneered the use of anthropological concepts for a better understanding of ancient Greece, intimated that between Homeric times and the fifth century BC, Greek society developed "from shame culture to guilt culture" (17). This is not borne out by Phaidra's psychology as shaped by Euripides when the fifth century was drawing to its close. Of course, such concepts must be handled with extreme caution, especially when dealing with literary characters, which are, after all, but verbal artefacts. Shame is the result of public disapproval. Yet the fear of being shamed acts as an inner brake to undesirable impulses: this element is certainly prominent in Phaidra. The sense of guilt, however, results from a transgression of prohibitions so thoroughly internalized that they are experienced as unquestioned absolutes which need neither rational justification nor the presence of an audience, real or imagined. Such a sense of guilt is an emotion unconnected with any fear of social ostracism or even of actual misdeeds. While successful concealment allows the evil-doer to escape scot-free of shame, the guilt-ridden individual is so tormented by his conscience's irrepressible injunction that he must (in Margaret Mead's words) "repent and *atone* for his *sin*" (494), even if it has remained unexposed. If the need to atone for one's sin is the acid test by which the presence of a sense of guilt can be gauged, then, obviously, Phaidra does not show the slightest trace of guilt feelings. This is precluded by the mere fact that Euripides has her commit suicide immediately after conceiving the evil scheme which, to her, is simply the most apposite manner of preserving her good name.

In the last decades there has been growing consensus among scholars that *Hippolutos* should be regarded as a problem play. Euripides shaped Phaidra's character and fate in such a way as to define in dramatic terms a problem which seems to have been very much on the minds of the intellectual élite in late-fifth-century Athens. Christian Wagner's recent statement that "in Phaidras Handeln kritisiert Euripides das Ethos seiner Zeit" (42) was anticipated by Charles Segal in 1970: "Through Phaedra's concern with appearance, reputation, the 'outside' world, Euripides raises the questions beginning to be asked in his time about the adequacy of an ethic based entirely upon external, social sanctions." Some fifty years ago von Erffa, in his pioneering study of *aidôs*, made the point that Euripides was the first to emphasize the ambiguity of the concept, to question its sovereignty and to vilify indiscriminate concern with reputation and public opinion (171). What matters, however, is not whether Euripides was the first, but that he was not the only one among a generation that included Socrates and Democritus. Little remains of this mental effervescence because Athens at the time was still largely an oral society. Of Socrates' fellow philosophers belonging roughly to the same period as Euripides, only fragments have been preserved. These, together with Greek tragedy, are merely the visible tip of an iceberg of abstract, rational meditation on man's nature, life and fate, which has vanished for ever.

Throughout these vestigial writings, however, there runs a thread of coherence which should make it possible to reconstruct a tentative approximation of the intellectual mood of the time. In his essay on "Shame and Purity in Euripides' *Hippolytus*", Segal called attention to a gnomic fragment ascribed to Democritus, in which the Sophist, who was about twenty years younger than Euripides, shows himself "concerned with finding moral restraint and moral order within the individual self rather than in the opinions of others" and claims that people should refrain from doing what is wrong, whether it will be revealed or remain undivulged: the wrong-doer should first and foremost feel shame in his own eyes (B 84).[7] The idea of self-shame recurs significantly in Democritus' preserved fragments. The word does raise semantic problems, as when Democritus describes the capacity to feel shame (*to aideisthai*, often translated as "the sense of honour"), as a precondition for "virtue" (here *aretê*), which in turn generates *aidôs*, variously rendered in modern translations as "honour" or "reverence" (B 179); this word might refer to outward marks of esteem, or to the person's contingent self-satisfaction at deserving public approval. There is no doubt, however, that Democritus was reacting against the supremacy of *eukleia*; in his yearning for internal criteria of righteousness, he was attempting the difficult task of defining a sanction of inwardness that would be more compelling than the social sanctions of legal punishment and public appraisal: "Virtue" (here: *agathon*) does not consist in abstaining from criminal deeds, but in not even willing them (B 62, B 68). He might have been thinking of the Nurse in *Hippolutos* when he observed that a person who refrains from evil solely out of fear for outward sanctions will do evil when secrecy ensures impunity (B 181).

In his discussion of shame and guilt Milton Singer noted that there exist "'inner' forms of shame paralleling almost exactly the forms of guilt" since they "may also be without any conscious reference to an audience, and need involve only the anxiety of failing to live up to one's ideals" (52). Obviously, the concept of inner shame, whether in Democritus' formulation, or as defined by modern psychoanalysis, takes us to a hazy area of moral experience, where it has not yet been possible to make a clear-cut distinction between inwardness and outwardness. It might be argued that it is relevant to Phaidra's mood at the very beginning of the play, when she blames herself for the "stain in her heart" whereas no one can possibly suspect her criminal passion. It is this, presumably, which accounts for C.C. Willink's assertion that Phaidra is deterred from adulterous indulgence "partly by a virtuous

---

[7] Democritus quotations refer to Hermann Diels' edition of pre-Socratic fragments.

instinct (which she disparages) but to a large extent by the certainty that she could not 'get away with it'".

In 1970 Segal, too, expatiated on the Queen's "inner purity", her "inward sense of modesty, shame, chastity", and even her sense of "an individual, private ethic, which may be more demanding than society itself". It is tempting to exaggerate the importance of inner shame in her psycho-ethical make up, and to read premonitions of later notions of moral excellence into the old tragedy. Such an interpretation is hardly warranted by the text. The confusion in Phaedra's mind and her tragic fate as designed by Euripides should rather be taken as a product and as an illustration of a transitional phase, a negative moment in the development of Greek thought. The traditional criterion of righteousness was crumbling.

The conflation of Euripides' dramatic theme and Democritus' apothegmatic speculations suggests that they were both responding to a preoccupation of wider import than mere individual queries. In the *polis*, the new Athenian society that had been taking shape for more than a century, the old Homeric concept of moral rectitude was bound to evaporate. The problem of assessing the relevance of public appraisal as a touchstone for moral action is likely to have been discussed widely by thoughtful citizens. In 431 BC, Euripides had his Medea exclaim, as she is about to take revenge on her husband by killing their children: "I know what evil I intend to do, but my fury is stronger than my will" (1078-79). Three years later, Phaedra turned this into a general statement: "We know what is right, but fail to carry it out" (380-81). The playwright was in his early fifties, Socrates in his early forties and Democritus in his early thirties. They were all addressing the same problem, but whereas the dramatist was voicing his puzzlement through his characters, the two younger men were trying to frame some sort of abstract solution: Democritus concocted the concept of self-shame; Socrates the notion that in wise men rational knowledge necessarily entails virtuous action.[8]

These were but preliminary steps towards the elaboration of an articulate doctrine of ethical valuation based on other than external criteria, and towards the emergence of a guilt culture. Such processes,

---

[8] Bruno Snell's 1948 discussion of a possible "controversy" between Euripides and Socrates is based on Xenophon's *Memorabilia*, (3,9,4) and Plato's *Protagoras*, (352 D). See also the essays by J. Moline and D. Claus.

however, are extremely slow. Greek philosophy as an articulate system was still in its infancy; indeed, Phaidra's passion, crime and death, had been part of its birth pangs. Plato and Aristotle were still to bring their contribution, but total indifference to the external sanctions of the honour/shame code of *aidôs* was not to be systematically advocated until the Hellenistic period, when the Stoa preached, as Albin Lesky put it, that it is "man's task to contribute to the firm rule of Logos in the world by bringing his own moral actions into correspondence with the great universal law which controls the cosmos, by repressing the irrational impulses of passion" (676). More than four centuries after Euripides, Rome's most prominent exponent of the Stoic doctrine, Seneca, was in his turn to dramatize the Phaidra story. Not surprisingly the Latin writer, while preserving the by now traditional characters and most of the essentials of the plot, altered the tale in major ways to suit his own purpose.

2

REASON AND GUILT: SENECA'S *PHAEDRA* (FIRST CENTURY AD)

Why did Seneca decide to postpone his own Phaedra's suicide until after Hippolytus' death? The question is by no means as futile as it may sound. Indispensible as source studies may be to trace the origin of a writer's materials and to locate him in a definite tradition, his departures from inherited patterns provide invaluable information concerning his individual outlook and intention. The father-wife-stepson triangle is liable to a variety of ethical analyses and dramatic treatments. Seneca's handling of the situation was bound to differ from Euripides', were it only because he was writing in and for a widely different society. He addressed a Roman intelligentsia that was cognizant of the Greek legacy. His readers knew the plays of Euripides. They were aware of the momentous developments that had immeasurably enriched Greek philosophy in the course of the five centuries since the death of the Greek playwright. They had assimilated many concepts for which Euripides and his contemporaries had been merely groping. Seneca himself was a prominent figure in the Stoic movement, which had outgrown the shame-culture outlook that early Greek thinkers had been striving to overcome. For a philosopher of his calibre to use the Phaedra tragedy as a weapon targeted at the honour code as Euripides' heroine understood it would have been redundant. Whether the Latin writer drew his inspiration, as some believe, from Euripides' first *Hippolutos* or from some other, perhaps oral, tradition, the many changes that he brought to the very texture of the story are by no means haphazard. All alterations are clues to the specificity of the thought underlying the dramatic action.

The first significant change occurs conspicuously at the beginning of the play as the audience is presented with two divergent interpretations of Phaedra's plight and consequently of the tragedy itself.

In her very first speech Phaedra accounts for her illicit passion as a manifestation of "the evil spell that bound [her] mother", Pasiphae (113-14). In Euripides she was merely the chosen instrument for Aphrodite's vengeance against Hippolutos. Seneca follows Ovid's *Heroids* (IV, 54 ff.) in attributing this curse to Venus' hatred of "all the tribe of Phoebus", especially "the daughters of the house of Minos" (126-27).[1] The human problem, the Phaedra-Hippolytus relationship, is no longer a consequence of the rivalry between two goddesses, which provided Euripides with a sort of frame action. It occupies a more definitely central position. Like her Greek model, however, the Latin Phaedra perceives herself as the powerless victim of a *fatale malum* (113), a fatal evil imposed upon her by a supernatural power. At least, that is how she describes herself to the Nurse; that is the way she wants the latter to view her predicament. There is no outward confirmation to guarantee Phaedra's sincerity: Seneca dispensed with Euripides' Prologue, in which Aphrodite herself describes her vengeful scheme. It is therefore conceivable that the Latin Phaedra's statement may be mere pretence.

Indeed, her self-analysis is immediately contradicted by the Nurse, who offers an alternative, less flattering interpretation of the Queen's infatuation with her stepson. This, she asserts, is by no means similar to Pasiphae's "monstrous", unnatural attraction to the Minotaur, which was inscribed in her fate; on the contrary, Phaedra's contemplated adultery-cum-incest is a source of greater infamy because it is a matter of conduct in which she indulges willingly: "monstra fato, moribus scelera imputes" (144). In the older woman's eyes, the Queen is a free agent, fully responsible for her own behaviour; she is all the more grievously mistaken in attributing her criminal passion to some supernatural power as the notion that love is a god, the son of Venus, is a mere piece of fiction invented by human lewdness as a convenient alibi (195-203). The Nurse thus disposes of Phaedra's claim that she is the impotent, irresponsible victim of some supernatural agency. One of the functions of the play is to make clear which one of these two mutually exclusive views of Phaedra's character and situation is the correct one.

---

[1] Mythology offers several explanations for the sexual anomalies in the house of Minos. Seneca here relies on a Homeric tradition that Helios incurred Aphrodite's wrath when he revealed her affair with the god of war, Ares, to her unattractive husband, the lame god Hephaistos. She decided to take revenge on Helios' daughter by the nymph Crete, Pasiphae, wife of Minos and mother of Ariadne and Phaedra (*Odyssey*, 8, 266-367).

It has long been part of the critical tradition that any comparison between Euripides and Seneca must be detrimental to the Latin writer, mainly on account of his inflated rhetoric. Twenty years ago it was still possible for Henry and Walker to deprecate the Nurse's lengthy didactic speech (128-77) as "highly inadequate", on the grounds that it is a trite mixture of maxims and apophthegms which have "no effect on the frenzied Phaedra nor any broader importance in the play" (225). Since then, Konrad Heldmann's brilliant analysis of 1974 (126-49) has decisively demonstrated the intellectual coherence of her discourse, at least until Phaedra utters her death-wish at line 254. It is my contention that the function of the *Nutrix* in this early section of the play is twofold: on a philosophical plane, she explicitly sets forth a moral outlook which closely corresponds to Stoic ethics; from a dramatic viewpoint, she forecasts with uncanny accuracy the entire development of the tragic action.

From the very first the Senecan *Nutrix* knows exactly what should be done in a situation that is not only immoral but also exceedingly dangerous. She unequivocally enjoins Phaedra to smother her flame ("extingue flammas", 131; "furorem siste", 248). Her immediate, spontaneous response is rooted in an ethical system, the key concept of which is *pudor*. The word, which is often translated as "shame" or "honour", occupies in Seneca's tragedy the same focal place as does *aidôs* in Euripides'. Yet, there is an important difference: unlike *aidôs*, *pudor* is not determined by outside appraisal. In other Senecan contexts this central principle of ethical valuation is dubbed *conscientia* and is clearly distinguished from public judgment; as the writer boasts in the *De vita beata*, "nihil opinionis causa, omnia conscientiae faciam" (20, 4, 5). In the play the word had first been used by Phaedra when she complained that neither fear nor conscience had deterred Theseus from his objectionable undertaking in the underworld: "Haud illum timor/Pudorque tenuit" (97). At a later point Theseus himself will speak of an *inscius pudor* (914), the unconscious moral instinct which keeps animals from violating (as he supposes Hippolytus to have done) the natural laws of sex and kinship. As a primal "instinct" that controls moral behaviour, *pudor* is a key concept, which the Nurse presently expounds in some detail.

In her view there are two degrees of *pudor*. The first is to will only honest things and never stray from the right way: "honesta primum est velle/nec labi via" (140), another formula for Seneca's oft-repeated notion that it is easier to check undesirable impulses at their inception than to control their full force; as he wrote in the *De ira*, "facilius est excludere perniciosa quam regere" (I, vii, 2). This first degree of *pudor*, which echoes Democritus, accounts for Phaedra's anxiety at her overruling passion, which she never describes as other than sinful (114) and impiously criminal ("nefas", 128). Her acknowledged powerlessness to repress her frenzy, alongside her envy of her mother, whose love was requited (119-23), are evidence that she has already fallen a prey to what the Nurse likewise describes as "impious things" ("nefanda", 130): she cannot refrain from desiring dishonest things, and she knows it. The Nurse therefore falls back on the second degree of pudor: "et secundum nosse peccandi modum" (141).

The meaning of *modum* is by no means obvious and the cryptic phrase has generated arcane controversies among translators and critics. At first sight it may seem that the Senecan nurse simply follows the pragmatism of her Greek model, who requested the Queen, as a second favour ("deutera charis", *Hipp* 508), to rely upon her advice, based as it is on her long experience and the *mêden agan* principle. E.F. Watling translates as "know where sin must stop", and Walter Poetscher is also of the opinion that the woman pragmatically advises the Queen not to go too far. But for others the scope of this statement is definitely intellectual: in Léon Herrmann's French rendering, the Nurse calls upon the Queen to "avoir conscience de l'étendue [*Ausmass* in Theodor Thomann's German translation] de sa faute", to be aware of the extent of her sin. The context, however, provides sufficient clarification: to explain what "nosse neccandi modum" means is exactly what the Nurse proceeds to do, as she lists with pitiless logic the sanctions to which Phaedra's contemplated misdeed is liable.

Nowhere, perhaps, is Seneca's skill in adapting his source material to his own ends better in evidence. The *Nutrix* begins by seemingly offering an enlarged version of the Greek Phaidra's own dismay as the latter foresees (but only *after* her Nurse's unsuccessful attempt) that her stepson in his anger is bound to reveal her sin to Theseus and ultimately to fill the land with her shame (*Hipp* 689-92). In Seneca this is presented indirectly *by the Nurse* in hypothetical form: supposing that Phaedra believes ("si credis", 145-46; "crede", 147; "credamus", 152; "credis", 157) that Theseus will not come back from the underworld and that her father, Minos, can be kept in ignorance, she can hardly expect to conceal her crime from her grandfather, the Sun, or from the father of the gods,

Jupiter. And even if she believes that her divine ancestors will be willing to gloss over her "infamous copulations" ("coitus nefandos", 150), even so (and here comes the climax, 162-63), there remains a court of last instance that cannot be abused

> ... poena praesens, conscius mentis pavor
> animusque culpa plenus et semet timens,

the inward condemnation, the built-in punishment, the gnawing voice of conscience, the self-inflicted disapproval, in which it is easy to recognize the torments of "guilt" in the psychoanalytical sense of the word.

Before once more calling on Phaedra to smother her passion the woman concludes the argument with a maxim: "scelus aliqua tutum, nulla securum tullit" (164), in which *tutum* refers to safety from public revelation and physical punishment, and *securum* to the unassailable inner peace of innocence. The dramatic relevance of her warning will emerge as the play goes on: Phaedra will ignore the Nurse's advice; she will succeed in deceiving Theseus; her Olympian family will remain conspicuously indifferent. To all practical purposes the Queen will be entirely safe (*tuta*); yet, she will not be *secura*: her conscience will drive her to self-denunciation and suicide. Meanwhile, the immediate, conscious purpose of the Nurse is to teach Phaedra *peccandi modum*, to impress on her mind the variety of sanctions she is likely, and ultimately certain, to suffer. The unspoken assumption underlying her discourse is that such knowledge will bring the Queen back to virtue. This, in fact, points to the main theme of the play: Phaedra's tragedy is a case study designed to test one of the basic premises of Stoic thought, that correct knowledge automatically entails virtuous behaviour, a recurring commonplace in Seneca's philosophical writings.[2]

The clash between these two antagonistic views of Phaedra's plight comes to a head in the ensuing dialogue. The root of the problem is encapsulated in Phaedra's assertion that although she realizes the truth in the woman's words, her frenzy prevents her from heeding the voice of reason: "Quae memoras scio/vera esse ... sed furor cogit sequi peiora. /Quid ratio possit? Vicit ac regnat furor" (177-84). The discussion becomes increasingly heated, until the *Nutrix* emotionally implores

---

[2] Examples are plentiful; see e.g. *Ep*. lxvi, 31-32 and lxxvii, 15-16.

Phaedra to put an end to her mad passion (257). The dialectical opposition between passion (*furor*) and the joint forces of *pudor* and *ratio* undergoes an abrupt change in the unexpected double conversion at the close of Act I. Phaedra announces that she is now convinced: though she cannot control her love, she has not lost her *pudor* and wants to keep her reputation unsullied; the only rational way out is to die: "Haec sola ratio est, unicum effugium mali" (354). The devoted Nurse is thunderstruck and instantly changes her mind: she forgets all about *pudor* and *ratio*; in her concern with the Queen's life and happiness, she advises her not to worry about public opinion ("contemne famam", 278), and she joins her Greek model in announcing that she will speak to Hippolytus.

The Nurse's change of mind, inspired by her deep love for the Queen, requires no comment. On the contrary, Phaedra's own change of mind has provided occasion for two types of interpretation. It is tempting to take her words at their face value, to assume with Leeman that they signal a genuine "change of attitude" prepared for by the foregoing debate, and that "after the paroxysm of feeling she suddenly recognized her true state of mind" (206).[3] After all, Phaedra now takes over from the Nurse in expounding Stoic theory. Her very words echo Seneca's own view that it is right to commit suicide in order to avoid evil: "bene autem mori est effugere mali periculum".[4] Roman readers familiar with Seneca's ideas would not fail to observe, however, as Pierre Grimal has done in more recent times, that one of the arguments put forward by Phaedra is mere concern with her good name — "motif impur pour un stoicien". Although the French scholar, who entertains a highly favourable view of Phaedra, seems to think that this concern is the "principale raison de sa résolution", it is conceivable that Seneca deliberately introduced this lapse in philosophical consistency in order to cast doubt at her sincerity in this juncture. The fact that her about-face lacks psychological plausibility further justifies Zintzen's blunt description of her otherwise moving speech as a "feigned death-wish" (97), a trick (34), targeted at the old woman, who finds herself suddenly threatened with her beloved Queen's suicide.

---

[3] This view has been put forward by Croisille, 288; Vretska, 167; Seidensticker, 100; Heldmann (1974), 152-61; and Davis, 121, among others.

[4] *Ep.* xxiv, lxx, and lxxvii. On the Stoic view of death and suicide, see Pohlenz, I, 323 and also Regenbogen, Bodson and Noyes.

The problem of Phaedra's sincerity is central. As Heldmann forcefully insisted, our whole understanding of the drama depends upon the answer we give to this question (1974, 154): did Seneca mean her utterance truly to convey what she has in mind? Or is it to be taken as a brilliant example of what present-day jargon calls the "perlocutionary use" of language?[5] Does she really intend to kill herself, or is she bent on frightening the old woman into discarding her lofty principles and altering her well-meant advice? The very ambiguity of Phaedra's discourse at the end of Act I intimates that the tragedy should not be regarded as a parable designed to illustrate the truth of some preconceived theory, but as a problem play that works out the seeming contradiction between Stoic dogma and the stark evidence that correct knowledge does not necessarily lead to virtuous behaviour.

Although Phaedra laments the powerlessness of her *ratio* to overcome her *furor*, unlike Euripides' Phaedra she is a woman of uncommon intellectual power. As was pointed out by Eckhard Lefèvre, each character in the play has a rapport of his own to knowledge and self-knowledge: Hippolytus does not care whether his misogynous frenzy derives from nature, reason or his own *furor* (567); Theseus is complacently unaware of his own obtuseness; as to the Nurse, who starts as a mouthpiece for Seneca, within a few minutes, as Pratt notes, she "preaches Stoic virtue to Phaedra and urges indulgence upon Hippolytus" (231). Phaedra's character is exceptional in that she is constantly aware of the wrongness of her conduct; obviously it is not beyond the mental power of this woman to indulge in some Machiavellian manipulating: by conjuring up a lurid variety of dying procedures (259-260), she successfully impresses the concrete significance of her alleged resolution upon the imagination of the *Nutrix*. What is more, this momentous peripeteia sets a recurrent pattern: on two more decisive occasions she will again proclaim her eagerness to die, only to stay obstinately alive, the Nurse acting in either case as a peg on which she hooks her pretexts for procrastinating.

---

[5] In the speech-act theory, a "perlocutionary act" is, in Walter Ong's definition, "one producing intended effects in the hearer, such as fright, conviction or courage" (170).

From the Nurse's opening speech in Act II (360-86), reader and audience are apt to infer that Phaedra has lost such composure as she exhibited during the high-flying discussion of Act I. The extreme disorder in her words and behaviour as she next briefly appears on-stage (387-403) testify to a state of disturbance, torn as she is between the rival demands of *furor* on one hand, *ratio* and *pudor* on the other. Her ostentatious confusion reaches its apex when she comes back at the end of the Nurse's inconclusive interview with Hippolytus: she faints (585-92), or perhaps pretends to do so.

As she recovers consciousness and finds herself almost in her stepson's arms, she is the one who utters the command ("endure your love", *Hipp* 476) that Euripides had attributed to the Nurse: "Aude, anime, tempta, perage mandatum tuum" (592). The phrase "execute your mandate" carries unambiguous intimations of a premeditated assignment. At this point Phaedra has clearly reverted to the mood that prevailed before her alleged death-wish, thus confirming that the latter was mere pretence, a tactical semblance of retreat in a continued strategy of seduction and self-indulgence. Speaking to herself, she determinedly gives up any attempt to obey her moral conscience: "serus est nobis pudor" (595). She even contemplates the possibility, should Theseus fail to reappear, of marrying her stepson as this would conceal, though not cancel, her crime: "iugali crimen abscondam face" (597). In an adaptation of the Greek Nurse's disillusioned observation, "Had I succeeded, I had been a wise one" (*Hipp* 700), Phaedra hopefully notes that success can make some crimes honourable: "honesta quaedam scelera successus facit" (598). Her final self-exhortation before she addresses Hippolytus, "go ahead, my soul" ("incipe, anime", 599), betrays her fully conscious determination to disregard the claims of both *ratio* and *pudor* and make what she hopes will be a successful attempt to gratify her lust.

This is a major departure from Euripides' pattern. Following, perhaps, a more archaic tradition which may have inspired *Hippolutos kaluptomenos* and was certainly closer to the Genesis pattern, Seneca has Phaedra herself convey her feelings and desires to her stepson in person. This alteration places her character in a new light. The failure of Euripides' heroine was of an intellectual order: her understanding did not reach further than her own puzzlement. She was aware of the equivocal nature of *aidôs*, but pursued *eukleia* in good faith and with flawless consistency. Seneca, however, makes his Phaedra responsible for whatever she says and does. By transferring to her some of the Greek Nurse's flashes of cynical insight and pragmatic advice he enhances the audience's perception of her unwavering awareness of right and wrong: she embarks on her evil course of action in full knowledge that she is violating the rational-ethical principles that should govern human conduct.

Characteristically, when Phaedra addresses the young Prince, she displays (or feigns) a different type of confusion. Forgetting (or pretending to forget) that she has just spurred herself on to speak out fearlessly ("intrepida constent verba", 503), she demurely claims that although a strong voice urges her to utter her feelings, a stronger voice is keeping her from speaking out (603). But this allegedly stronger voice, which is the voice of *pudor* and *ratio*, turns out to be weaker than the voice of *furor* since she goes on to declare her love with unparalleled rhetorical skill; this contradicts her bashful conclusion with its blasphemous invocation assuring the gods that she does not want what she wants: "Vos testor omnis, caelites, hoc quod volo/me nolle" (604-605). Since Zerlina in Mozart's *Don Giovanni* used the same conceit ("vorrei e non vorrei", I, iii), it has been common knowledge that this kind of statement conveys a coy helplessness that is but a prelude to graceful yielding! Phaedra knows very well what it is that she wants, and she sets out to get it with unrelenting single-mindedness.

The ending of Act II runs parallel to that of Act I. The Nurse had taught that Phaedra's lust should be repressed; Hippolytus makes it clear that it shall not be gratified. The Queen restates her awareness that she is unable to suppress her evil passion ("furor cogit sequi/peiora", 178-79; "fugienda petimus", 699). She re-emphasizes the impotence of reason ("quid ratio possit?", 184; "mei non sum potens", 699). Her conclusion in Act I had been that she must die ("decreta mors est", 259); now, as Hippolytus draws his sword in disgust and anger, she exclaims that her highest wish is now fulfilled since she will die at the hand of her beloved, with her *pudor* intact ("salvo pudore", 712). It should be noted that at the very moment when the Greek Phaidra is most strongly alarmed about her honour-as-reputation (*eukleia*) since her stepson is now informed, her Latin counterpart is conveniently forgetting her earlier recognition that her moral integrity (*pudor*) is a thing of the past (595); nor does she evince any preoccupation with honour-as-reputation (*fama*).

Such lowly considerations as Phaedra's life and fame are at best worthy of the Nurse's attention. As Hippolytus departs, thoughtlessly leaving his sword behind, the faithful servant, faced with imminent disaster, forgets her lofty principles and edifying disquisitions. She instantly thinks up a trick of her own to turn the tables on the young Prince. She calls all Athens ("adeste, Athenae", 725) to witness that he has been trying to rape his stepmother. While she sets out to revive Phaedra from her new faint ("recipe iam sensus", 733), she assures her with soothing disingenuousness that it is the mind's intention, not the facts of the case, that makes a woman unchaste (735).

Many commentators take it for granted that Phaedra is reluctantly compelled to embrace the unpalatable role now devised for her by the Nurse. There is indeed reason to speculate that her antics at the end of Act II are not genuine: her anger at Hippolytus' contemptuous rebuff, the depth of her disillusionment, the intensity of her emotional and sexual frustration, can easily account for her torn, dishevelled hair, her breast-beating described by the Nurse (731-34), for the lamentations, the cries and tears, the grief and sorrow soon to be observed by Theseus (850-53). Act III, however, shows that she is able to enlist such outward signs of defeat and helplessness in the service of the Nurse's scheme with what even Remo Giomini does not hesitate to call "fredda e calcolata risoluzione" (73). Such an abrupt turn around, leading ultimately to the death of the man Phaedra is supposed to be in love with, cannot be presented with any dramatic plausibility unless the playwright provide some indication of the steps through which the character must needs pass. This transition appears unobtrusively at the end of the Chorus' lengthy, rambling, apparently mostly irrelevant *canticum*:

> Quid sinat inausum feminae praeceps furor?
> Nefanda juveni crimina insonti apparat.
> En scelera! Quaerit crine lacerato fidem,
> decus omne turbat capitis umectat genas:
> instruitur omnis fraude femina dolus.
> (824-28)

(Is there no end to the audacity of a woman crazed with passion?
She prepares to charge the innocent young man with a heinous crime.
What infamy! She seeks evidence in her tangled hair,
she mars the beauty of her head, she stains her face with tears.
The whole plot is prepared with womanish astuteness.)

Grimal (1965, 123 n) and even Zintzen (88-89 n) find it *étonnant* and *sonderbar* that the Chorus should be able to forecast what Phaedra is going to do in the next Act. It seems more economical to understand that the Chorus is accurately describing what is happening off-stage and inside the Queen's mind for the benefit of the audience:[6] Phaedra is recovering from the shock, she has adhered to the Nurse's scheme, she prepares to play her part in the deceitful plot by taking advantage of the disordered appearance in which her miserable failure has left her.

Both women, however, are understandly nonplussed at Theseus' sudden, unexpected return from hell. To his anxious questions about the cause of the cries and tears that he hears, the Nurse can only reply that the Queen has resolved to die, that she is dying — on account, she adds cryptically, of his return. Phaedra then appears, Hippolytus' sword in her hand. She, too, seems to be in disarray. To Theseus' increasingly heated questions she gives equally dark answers, perhaps in the hope of gaining time in order to collect herself. She does not bring herself to "confess" the "truth" until her husband in his extreme anger threatens to have the Nurse beaten for her secret. This passage deserves deeper scrutiny than it has usually been awarded. It is often assumed that Phaedra "confesses" Hippolytus' alleged crime in order to save the Nurse from Theseus' wrath. In his edition Grimal claims that the threat constrains her to "commettre le crime devant lequel elle recule, mais vers lequel la fatalité la pousse" (130). More likely it is not "fate" or even compassion for the Nurse that prompts her, but sheer self-interest, what Segal calls "her instinct for survival" (1986, 167). She cannot but be mindful that her husband is not noted for forbearing patience: the Nurse herself has reminded her that he murdered Hippolytus' mother even though she had been loyal to him (226-27). If Phaedra is to survive, she must leave nothing to chance. In fact, her premeditation has just been exposed by the Chorus. What she has to fear is that the Nurse under torture might tell the real truth, not the fiction hastily concocted in lines 719-33. This is the reason why she hastens to deliver the mendacious report in person.

---

[6] This point was convincingly made by Konrad Heldmann in his comparative study of Seneca's Phaedra and her Greek models (114).

Her brief speech is a masterpiece of disingenuousness. She begins with a blasphemy, calling to witness Jupiter and the Sun, who, she recalls, is the origin of her lineage. She insists on the successful resistance of her will (*animus*) to her alleged aggressor's prayers and threats. She declares that her body had to yield to violence. Finally, in a seeming re-enactment of the Lucretia story as recently recounted by Livy (I, 58, 7-10),[7] she forcefully announces her intention to wash her honour clean with her own blood: "Labem hanc pudoris eluet noster cruor" (893). The audience cannot fail to note that this monstrous piece of slander, while it may save Phaedra's life and reputation, nullifies any pretensions she may have to *pudor* as moral integrity. As in the Phaedra-*Nutrix* scene at the beginning, her alleged *libido moriendi* is designed to bring pressure, this time upon Theseus, who has to be convinced of his wife's stainless virtue and unimpeachable sincerity.

After conveying her appalling message, Phaedra, unlike her Greek model, obstinately goes on living despite her disclaimers. Nor will she reappear, or indeed be mentioned again, until Act V, some 250 lines later, after Theseus' garrulous speech, the Chorus' lengthy *canticum* and her stepson's gory death. She has set the devilish machinery in motion and can safely depart — presumably to start experiencing, as the Nurse has predicted, the pangs of her conscience, "conscius mentis pavor" (162).

The legend describes Theseus as enterprising, courageous and oversexed, but not as inordinately clever. In the Senecan play, while Phaedra is as perceptive and weak-willed as Macbeth, he is as gullible as Othello. He takes his wife's statement at face-value and proceeds forthwith to have his son duly and terminally castigated. Seneca emphasizes this point with savage irony by having the poor man intone portentous generalities on the theme of appearance and reality:

> O vita fallax! abditos sensus geris
> animisque pulchram turpibus faciem induis.
> Pudor impudentem celat, audacem quies,
> pietas nefandum: vera fallaces probant
> simulantque molles dura.
> (918-22)

---

[7] See Elżbieta Olechowska's comments on echoes from Livy's Lucretia story in *Phaedra*.

> (O deceitful life! you hide your true leanings
> and conceal your foul soul under a fair mask.
> Lechery masked by modesty, boldness by moderation,
> impiety by devoutness: liars feign truthfulness
> and wantons austerity.)

The whole inflated speech is meant by Theseus as a comment on Hippolytus' alleged misdeeds, but it would be a dumb audience that did not perceive how cogently the description applies to Phaedra.

A sense of ironic ambivalence is maintained through the Chorus: the ensuing *canticum* is an elegiac-philosophical lament on the fact that Nature and Jupiter, who successfully exercise joint control over the orderliness of the physical world, fail to enforce moral order in the affairs of man: they do not bother to reward the good ones or punish the bad ones ("non sollicitus/prodesse bonis, nocuisse malis", 975-76). Theseus' *vita fallax* motif is thus transferred from the epistemological level of perception to the ethical level of action and justice: lust defeats the pure (980), the powerful are perfidious (981), virtue is not rewarded (984-85), poverty is the prize of the chaste and vice makes the adulterous powerful (985-87). The depressing conclusion: virtue (*pudor*) is useless, honours (*decus*) are deceitful (987-88). As no names are mentioned, the Chorus' lament could easily be mistaken for a sample of the conventional claptrap to which "philosophical" pessimism is liable in crude minds. An attentive audience, however, is bound to wonder whom the Chorus have in mind when speaking of *boni* and *mali*. Léon Herrmann noted long ago that "les allusions du choeur à l'injustice dont Hippolyte va être victime sont très nettes" (215); they are not more explicit, however, than the allusions to the seeming triumph of Phaedra at this stage in the development of the dramatic action.

Seneca's consummate artistry has propelled the reader or spectator to an acme of uncertainty, especially if they have the Euripides tradition in mind, in which case they may pardonably suppose that Phaedra is quietly hanging herself off-stage.

But what about the ideal reader or spectator, the unlikely innocent creature, who reads or sees *Phaedra* for the first time and has never heard of Euripides, or Sophocles, or Ovid, he for whom each writer, in his own utopian innocence, displays his talent? As Act IV comes to its sorrowful close, this improbable creature is equally likely to think that the play is over and that the bloody Queen has escaped scot-free. After all, none of the Nurse's unpleasant predictions in 145-61 has materialized: Theseus has so much confidence in his wife's loyalty that he has had his son murdered; Phaedra's father, Minos, has given no sign of his allegedly "sagacious care" (152); her ancestor Phoebus and Jupiter himself have proved singularly indifferent to her impudently blasphemous invocations; Neptune's lethal intervention has just confirmed that the "favour of the gods" (159) conspires to conceal her impious passion and deeds; the Nurse herself has unobtrusively vanished from the cast. Clearly, in the topsy-turvy world described by Theseus and the Chorus ("Res humanas ordine nullo/fortuna regit", 977-78), the lewd Queen's astuteness has given her complete impunity: her life and reputation are now safe (*tuta*) from any outward, physical or social, sanctions. What is it, then, in Seneca's dramatic intention, that prompts her to come back, with Hippolytus' sword still in hand, in her by now customary distraught ("furor", 1156) and noisy ("vociferatio planctusque", 1157-58) manner? It is in order to raise this question and provide an answer that Seneca discarded Euripides' timing of the Queen's suicide and allowed her to outlive Hippolytus.

Henry and Walker ungraciously asserted that Phaedra's last speech is nothing more than "a chaotic series of sentences" that show her "unable despite her efforts to establish coherence in her own mind" (218). It is true that her slightly disjointed discourse betrays her agitated mood. Yet from the point of view of dramatic art, it is imperative that this final act of the play should clarify the issue, especially now that Seneca has created a climax of almost unbearable suspense. It is therefore desirable to disentangle the admittedly somewhat scrambled motivations of Phaedra in this her dying speech.

She has come to make a clean breast ("Me, me ... invade et in me monstra ... emitte", 1159-60). Her changed mood is due to the death of Hippolytus. It is reinforced by the sight of his torn body. Her *anagnorisis* illustrates Keats's dictum to the effect that "axioms in philosophy are not axioms until they are proved upon our pulses" (141-42). Throughout the play death has been abundantly present in the Queen's discourse, especially in the form of her feigned death-wish. Now, however, mortality has become a matter of raw experience: it has been proved upon her pulse with irrepressible urgency. All the more so as her passion for Hippolytus has by no means abated. Her rambling outbursts on this point are couched in virtually the same terms as her original love declaration in Act II: there is indeed a gradation from her earlier eagerness to follow him wherever he might go (613-16) through her willingness to follow him through fire and raging sea (700), to her present determination to accompany him across the Styx and through the lakes of Tartarus (1170-80) in the hope of joining their fates ("junxisse fata", 1184) in death. Yet, she remains acutely conscious that this adulterous, incestuous love is evil: she pounds at it with the same damning epithets that have been used throughout the play: *amens* (insane, 702, 1180), *demens* (mad, 202, 1193), and *nefas* (impious, 1186, 1192 and *passim*).

The continued intensity of this lawless passion interlocks with something that was clearly beyond the reach of Euripides' Phaidra: a sense of guilt in the modern, restricted meaning of the word. This sense of guilt has two components: remorse and atonement. Although Phaedra is not blind to Theseus' share of responsibility (1164-67, 1191-92, 1199-1200), she knows that the death of Hippolytus is primarily her own fault ("Hippolyte, tales intuor vultus tuos/talesque feci", 1168-69): it is seldom noted that she never tries to cast the blame on the Nurse, as the Greek Phaidra did and as Racine's Phèdre will do. Furthermore, she is also guilty of defiling her husband's bed with her unchaste yearnings (1185-86). These are the two unforgivable sins for which she must atone: she must die, not solely to placate her stepson's shadow (1181), but also because it would be unfair for her to return to Theseus as if she was a virtuous wife (1186-87). When she hails death as the only relief for her evil love ("O mors, amoris una sedamen mali", 1189), she echoes her earlier definition of death as "unicum effugium mali" (253), but the context of her mood is different: this is no feigned death-wish; she really means what she says. First of all, however, she must redress the injury done to Hippolytus' good repute: her "audite, Athenae" (1101) echoes the Nurse's public denunciation of the young man's alleged crime, "Adeste, Athenae!" (725). She then stabs herself and dies.

It has long been a critical commonplace that Seneca "does not aim at a consequent and logical action or at a coherent psychology in his characters" (Snell 1967, 26). There is no denying that the Phaedra of Act V is a very different person from what she was in the first three acts. Nor is this the only example of a shockingly abrupt psychological change in the play. The Queen's sudden conversion is a mirror image of the Nurse's equally sudden half-turn in Act I. When faced with the prospect of Phaedra's death, the good woman had promptly reneged on her unimpeachable theoretical principles; loving devotion was her motive. Conversely, Phaedra, who had done all she could to gratify a passion that she knew to be evil, finally comes to recognize the vital (and, consequently, deadly) truth of ethical principles of whose rationality she had always been aware. We are not shown the processes that must have occurred in her tormented mind when she was off-stage (735-1155). But while important inferences can be drawn from their outcome in Act V, a major clue was actually provided in the prophetic speech uttered by the Nurse before her moral insight was clouded by her unconditional dedication to her mistress's life and happiness. Theseus' gullibility and Hippolytus' death have indeed made the Queen safe (*tuta*) from any outward punishment. They have not made her safe in an absolute sense (*secura*): there is the "poena praesens" (162), the built-in sanction, the voice of conscience, the inner sense of guilt in a soul tormented by the gnawing awareness of her own crime. The only way to evade this most dreadful punishment is death, which will free her at one stroke from both life and her crime ("animaque Phaedram pariter ac scelere exuam", 1178). The suicide of Euripides' Phaidra was a clear example of shame-culture behaviour: her sole concern was to preserve her reputation. The suicide of Seneca's Phaedra is an early example of guilt-culture behaviour: repentance is the gist of her final rhesis, atonement is the purpose of her ultimate action.

Seneca's *Phaedra* is in itself an indication that the internalization of moral criteria which Attic thinkers had been striving for in the fifth century BC had gained considerable ground, at least in the minds of the intellectual élite, by the time Stoicism had begun to spread in Rome while Christianity was being born in the Middle East. This chronological coincidence is probably responsible for the inclination of many distinguished Senecan scholars to read eschatological significance into Phaedra's self-inflicted death, and to assume that death somehow effects a restoration of her honour and a redemption of her sinful soul. In the midst of her last speech, Phaedra, with bitterly subdued irony, hails death as "the greatest ornament of her wounded *pudor*" (1189), that is to say, dying is the most honourable and virtuous action left to her stained integrity. This was rendered in Herrmann's French translation as "O mort, qui peux le mieux *rendre l'honneur* à ma pudeur outragée". Some forty years later Pierre Grimal still insisted that Phaedra commits suicide "pour *retrouver* sa dignité" (1963, 314) and that "la mort *rend* à Phèdre son honneur" (1965, 160; italics added). Meanwhile, in 1952 Ettore Paratore had eloquently enlarged on this interpretation of Phaedra's physical death as spiritual redemption:

> In tutto questo patetico monologo ... non troveresti una parola che stoni coll'altezza umana ormai raggiunta dal personaggio di Fedra, *che non redima la sua passione*, pur nella sua colpevole torbizza, da ogni aspetto crudamente sensuale e non la sospinga nell'Olimpo dei grandi amori romantici (222-23; italics added).

Although this charitable view was approvingly quoted by Remo Giomini (105), nothing in the text warrants such an anachronistic, Christian-Romantic rewarding of Phaedra's self-destruction. Such misreading was presumably prompted by the impact of Phaedra's rhetoric in the first half of her speech, bolstering the pathos inherent in the situation. She views herself as a "star-crossed lover" and the climax of her apostrophe to Hippolytus — "et te ... sequar" (I shall still follow you, 1179-80) — can be taken by modern critics to anticipate Romeo's poignant soliloquy as he is about to drink poison in the vault of the Capulets: "I still [i.e. ever] will stay with thee" (V, iii, 105). Coming as they do immediately after her assertion that death will rid her both of life and of her crime, these words are an obvious *non sequitur*: they signal that Phaedra is bent on persevering in her lawless passion in Tartarus. One might even speculate that it is her own perception of this which prompts her to return, in the second part of the speech, to her original purpose: the full confession of her sins leading to self-inflicted punishment.

It is profoundly misleading and anachronistic to discuss Seneca's *Phaedra* in terms of spiritual redemption. The tragedy is a Stoic problem play staging the development of the conflict between a person's carnal instincts and the Stoic ideal of rational virtue. The antithesis is brought out all the more forcibly because of the heroine's penetrating intellect and unimpeachable moral judgement. Not only does her love frenzy compel her to act in contradiction to ethical principles to which she fully adheres in the abstract: it also makes use of those very principles to further its own unholy ends through clever manipulation of the Nurse and of Theseus. The first three acts trace Phaedra's graded steps downwards until the ultimate catastrophe to which her evil course has been leading; they firmly position her as a pathological case, an anomaly in a Stoic universe. Seneca then brings her to the verge of grasping the full extent of her deviation just before she utters the slanderous charge against the man she loves: when Theseus asked her what misdeed her death was to expiate, she darkly retorted, "Quod vivo" (880) — my being alive. The awesome truth of this flash of insight, however, is not proved upon her pulse with compelling immediacy until Hippolytus' death. This is the shock that allows her *pudor*, her moral conscience to take the upper hand and govern her behaviour in compliance with the Stoic doctrine of suicide: the fact that she dies by her own choosing in order to expiate her violation of virtue is in itself the ultimate triumph of reason.

If Phaedra's suicide cleanses the universe of the impurity that was her being alive, it does not follow that her honour is restored or her soul redeemed, much less her passion retroactively glorified. Nowhere does she express such expectations. Only her terminal deed of self-annihilation is honourable, virtuous and rational. That her virtue and her reputation have been destroyed beyond all hope of recovery is decisively notified in Theseus' baleful obituary lines:[8] they close the play with the order that Phaedra's contemptible body be buried deep under the earth, which shall lie heavy on her impious heart:

> ... Istam terra defossam premat
> gravisque tellus impio capiti incubet (1279-80).

Final condemnation could hardly be pronounced with more scathing scorn. Whatever his faults and weaknesses, Theseus, we must remember, is the highest-ranking person in the play. As Hans Herter pointed out, this is "das letzte Wort des Philosophendichters, das in uns nachhallen soll" (77). The tragedy of Seneca's Phaedra signals the triumph of a guilt ethic based on the primacy of reason and the inner sanctions of conscience just as the tragedy of Euripides' Phaidra had illustrated the failure of a shame ethic based on the primacy of reputation and the outward sanctions of society. Not until the spread of Christianity in the Western world was a new, "supernatural" parameter to be introduced into the situation.

---

[8] The opposite view is propounded in Anthony James Boyle's claim that "emphasis on Theseus' guilt (esp. 1201 ff., 1248 ff.) makes the final comment on Phaedra and its simplistic moral judgement abhorrent. The audience's increasing sympathy for Theseus reaches here its maximum point only to be switched suddenly by this brilliant ending back to Phaedra. Like Jason in the final lines of *Medea*, Theseus reveals that he has understood little."

3

THE ETHICS OF FEAR: BANDELLO'S *NOVELLA 44* (1554)

Bandello's mention of the Phaedra story in the 44th tale of his *Novelliere* is incidental, but it points to an analogy that is more than coincidental. Although the Italian story diverges from the Phaedra pattern in several respects, the same ingredients go to the making of the Ferrarese triangle. As father, husband and ruler, Marquis Niccolò d'Este demands as much respect as Theseus; his fifteen-year old wife, Parisina, is even more impudently neglected than Phaedra; she falls in love with her stepson, Ugo, who, unlike Hippolytus, succumbs to her blandishments: the classical Phaedra's role as the prime transgressor thus comes to be assumed by the young pair. However, there is enough similarity in situation and plot to make comparison possible and legitimate. Admittedly, Bandello's fiction does not fathom the psycho-ethical depths explored in the tragedies of Euripides and Seneca. Yet he enjoyed international fame in Western Europe in the sixteenth and seventeenth centuries. Many of his *novelle* were translated into French and Spanish, and the collection was used by Shakespeare and other Elizabethans in search of plots.[1] This suggests a measure of concordance with the Renaissance *Zeitgeist* in so far as a popular writer's interests and his audience's expectations can provide a clue to some of its main preoccupations.

Down-to-earth realism is of the essence of the *novella*, which, as developed by Boccaccio, purported to narrate real-life stories, thus gratifying the bourgeois reader's craving for factual information. In Bandello's description of Parisina's motivation, no mention is made of

---

[1] *Hamlet, Romeo and Juliet, Much Ado about Nothing* and *Twelfth Night* can be traced to Bandello or to his French translators and imitators, François de Belleforest and Pierre Boaistuau. Later luminaries such as Byron, Stendhal and Musset also sought inspiration in the *Novelliere*.

any metaphysical interference — any divine curse or, as a medieval writer would have chosen, any intervention of the devil. She is presented as a free agent, a Renaissance woman. Her primary motive is pride, bolstered by sexual frustration on account of the neglect she suffers at the hands of her husband:

> veggendo la marchesana che'l suo consorte era di cotal natura che per logorar quello di fuori risparmiava il suo, deliberò anch'ella non star con la mani a cintola e consumar la sua giovanezza indarno (518).

Among the eligible young men at court, the most attractive one, she discovers, is her own stepson, whose sight engulfs her in a burning flood of carnal passion.

Parisina does not immediately set out to seduce Count Ugo the way Potiphar's wife did and as Euripides' first Phaidra is generally supposed to have done. The counter-force that curbs her lust for a while is described as *vergogna*, which plays the same part in the inner structure of the story as do *aidôs* as *eukleia* in Euripides or *pudor* and *ratio* in Seneca. The word derives from the Latin *verecundia*. Like its equivalents in Spanish (*vergüenza*), Portuguese (*vergonha*) and French (*vergogne*), it is usually translated as "shame". It also connotes modesty and even mere bashfulness; in women it refers most importantly to chastity inspired by concern with public opinion and especially by a married woman's fear of losing her good name and destroying her husband's honour. It is characteristic of many shame cultures that although they do not require marital fidelity of men, they place a high premium on married women's chastity. Despite more than a thousand years of Christian teaching, a significant segment of Italian Renaissance society still entertained, or had reverted to, a typical shame-culture outlook in this and other respects. In *Il libro del cortegiano* (1528), Baldassare Castiglione had argued that although a dissolute life was neither a vice nor a fault nor a disgrace for a man, it was an everlasting source of opprobrium and shame ("obbrobrio e vergogna") in a woman (322). It is the fear of such disgrace that first keeps Parisina from openly confessing her lust to the young man, who remains blind to her lascivious manners: "la vergogna le annodava la lingua" (518).

The nature of the conflict in Parisina's mind is not really clarified when Bandello relates that after a time she realizes that nothing but her sense of shame ("la vergogna sola") prevents her from conveying her "love" to Ugo: no other possible cause for restraint has so far been mentioned, whether fear of physical punishment, or of divine retribution. It may be that Bandello intended the *marchesana*'s reasoning to be perceived as a perverted application of Aristotle's negative assessment of social honour as something external to man,[2] with which the truly virtuous should not be overly concerned. Anyhow, this observation whets her "disonesti e scelerati appetiti" (518), and prompts her to seduce Count Ugo as soon as an opportunity arises.

The occasion is offered when Niccolò is summoned to Milan by Duke Visconti. Driven by a "love that has put to flight all shame and respect" (519), Parisina in her turn summons the young man and expounds to him her plight, feelings and desires with extreme loquaciousness. In order to overcome the bewilderment of the count, who "had never thought of such wickedness", she then resorts to lewd kisses ("lascivissimamente basciandole", 521) in order to distract him from realizing the injury to his father and the danger he is running into. She goes to work with such expeditious skill that the young man, "feeling his thing grow" ("sentendosi crescer roba per casa", 521), cannot but allow sexual appetite to silence any moral or rational considerations. The frenzied nature of their carnal passion is thus made clear.

For two years the lovers quietly indulge their appetites unbeknown to anyone at court until a man-servant begins to spy on them and calls the unfortunate husband to witness their wicked frolics through a hole in the ceiling. The Marquis's "love for wife and son" turns to instant hatred. He forthwith decides to avenge his honour most ferociously. They are immediately imprisoned and, after three days, beheaded. As to the Marquis of Ferrara, he promptly sets about marrying another wife and producing another heir.

Neither Bandello nor his characters are very reflexive persons. There is no evidence of any inner conflict in Niccolò's mind. With as much haste as Theseus in the classical tragedies had decided on the fate of Hippolytus, Bandello's hero obeys the precepts of the honour code in its Italian version. Spanish honour demanded, to borrow a title of Calderón's, "secret vengeance for secret offence" — *A secreto agravio, secreta venganza*; in Italy, however, a man's slighted honour could only be properly restored through public punishment. In compliance with this requirement, when Niccolò orders the young lovers to be

---

[2] An in-depth discussion of this point will be found in the first chapter of Norman Council's *When Honour's at the Stake: Ideas of Honour in Shakespeare's Plays*.

imprisoned, he explains to all present the reason for his decision (523). He obeys the code spontaneously, without any qualms or questioning. To Bandello and his audience, the wronged husband's single-minded devotion to honour does not require any explaining. He simply does his duty. He does not even bewail the cruelty of the code, as will so many fathers and husbands in the Spanish Golden Age *comedia*.

Nevertheless, as the Marquis has his wife and his son put in chains, a new element is introduced both into the story and into the general pattern of the Phaedra syndrome: he sends each of them two friars so that they may prepare for death and save their souls. Bandello was a cleric, and a few years before the first volume of his *Novelliere* was published in Lucca, he had been appointed temporary Bishop of Agen (France). The Council of Trent had been at work for some ten years, preparing the Counter-Reformation. Therefore it is slightly surprising that until the final pages, neither Parisina or Ugo, nor, for that matter, Niccolò, ever mention God, the teachings of the Church or the sinful character of a passion that is so obviously both adulterous and incestuous. This may probably be regarded as a valuable indication of the relative importance of social and religious criteria in the ethical praxis of the time.

The overall impression is one of utter lack of logic. Bandello's objective narrative style allows not a word of condemnation for Niccolò's profligate sexual indulgence either before or after his marriage, and although his unfaithfulness is responsible for Parisina's own immorality, it provides no excuse for it: the slighted woman's manner of seeking compensation is consistently dubbed "dishonest", "lascivious" and "wicked" — a glaring manifestation of the enduring phallocratic trend in many Mediterranean shame cultures. No one seems to be aware of the antinomy between worldly honour as reputation and Christian honour as virtue, an important topic for Humanist thinkers of the Renaissance. While this antinomy was a matter for theoretical speculations, Bandello, his characters and, in all likelihood, his audience, take it for granted that this-worldly life is to be ruled by worldly criteria: anticipating Tirso de Molina's Don Juan, they assume that it will be time to think of the commands of God and the Church when they reach the threshold of the other world — oblivious of the fact that such presumption is in itself a sin against the theologal virtue of Hope. Their outlook should not prove puzzling in our Western society, which, though nominally Christian, has merely substituted money for honour as its highest principle of valuation. In shaping the character of Niccolò d'Este, Bandello naively failed to perceive — or chose not to evince — the key ethical problem on which Lope de Vega was to focus his dramatic attention in *El castigo sin venganza*. We do not know whether the historical Marquis of fifteenth-century fame actually showed such laudable concern for the salvation of his victims' souls.[3] If this particular incident was invented by Bandello, it should probably be ascribed to the writer's desire to compensate for his manifest relish in developing the erotic aspect of the anecdote by appending an edifying ending.

This admittedly conjectural interpretation finds some support in the two lovers' response to their condemnation. While they had been partners in transgression throughout the erotic central section of the story, their fate now forks into divergent attitudes, either of which is so exemplary as to sound contrived. Count Ugo spends the three-day interval in pious conversation with the holy monks: in preparation for "la meritata morte" he repents "con grandissima contrizione"; he implores God, his father and the world to pardon his sin and receives "devotamente il sacratissimo corpo del nostro Salvatore", thus ensuring the salvation of his immortal soul.

Parisina, on the contrary, remains close to the Senecan Phaedra model: she obstinately persists in her unbridled passion for her stepson; she notifies her husband that she alone is responsible for the offence, that she misled the young man, and that she alone should be punished for their joint crime (523); she proclaims her indifference to her imminent beheading. In Seneca such behaviour was described as the only honourable deed left to Phaedra. But since Bandello has been careful to insist that the friars' efforts to bring the *marchesena* to repentance were of no avail, that she refused to confess, that she showed no remorse at her wickedness, no doubt can be left in the reader's mind that Parisina is indeed headed for eternal torments in hell.

---

[3] This, however, is by no means implausible. Hauvette describes the main trends in the historical Niccolò III's character as "une grande dévotion jointe à une humeur violente, sanguinaire à l'occasion, et à un extraordinaire tempérament de don Juan" (19); he adds that the Marquis' devoutness was not to be equated with genuine faith and piety: it is "une des formes les plus basses de l'esprit religieux", made up of "crédulité" and "superstition" (21). It is true that in England and France the death penalty usually entailed denial of the sacraments so that the guilty should be aware that they were doomed to eternal damnation (Huizinga, 30). But Italians were probably more mindful of Pope Clement V's injunction of 1311 that criminals should be allowed to confess before being executed.

The structure of the *novella* is built on two contrasts: firstly, between the two main segments — the occasionally ticklish seduction scene and the response of the two lovers faced with death; secondly, between Parisina's literally unforgivable obstinacy in evil and Ugo's commendable willingness to confess and repent and accept his punishment. While romantic readers may admire Parisina for remaining indomitably true to her passion even at the cost of eternal damnation, there is no doubt that the writer upholds Ugo's edifying ending. This may have been intended as an orthodox justification for the somewhat scabrous story: as J.H. Plumb has aptly noted, "Bandello's stories, cast in moral guise, nevertheless read like the chronicle of a pornographer" (137). In the midst of the intellectual effervescence raised by Humanism, the Reformation and the Counter-Reformation, the writer may have found it inadvisable to indulge in wholesale advocacy of self-indulgence as Boccaccio had done two centuries earlier.

However, such self-contradictory attitudes need not be branded as sheer hypocrisy prompted by fear of ecclesiastical sanctions, harsh and frequent as these might be. Pietro Aretino, Bandello's contemporary and the author of the scurrilous *Ragionamenti* (1534-36), was also responsible for religious treatises and saints' lives. While recalling that the Renaissance intelligentsia was not affected by the kind of prudishness that was later to sway influential sections of Western society, it is more reasonable to speak of double-think rather than hypocrisy. When Le Maçon was commissioned to translate the *Decamerone* into French on the request of Marguerite de Navarre, the latter's brother, Francois I, granted him a privilege in order that the work might edify readers of good will and help them eschew vice and follow honour and virtue:

> affin que par la communication et lecture dudict livre les lecteurs d'icelluy de bonne volonté puissent acquérir quelque fruict de bonne edification; mesmement pour connoistre les moyens de fuyr à vices et suyvre ceux qui duisent à honneur et vertu (quoted by Toldo, 30-31).

The idea was that many seemingly scabrous stories actually illustrate the workings of what Thomas Rymer was later to dub "poetick justice": the writer needed simply to record facts showing that the virtuous are rewarded and the vicious duly chastised (the "law of compensating values" which lorded over Hollywood from the mid-1930s was likewise to specify that evil characters were acceptable in films as long as they were punished before the fade-out). No author's comment was necessary, as the readers could be expected to meditate on the significance of the "facts". Nevertheless, in her own stories, posthumously published as *L'Heptaméron* (1558-59), Marguerite de Navarre went a step further and appended to each of her tales a model of the kind of meditation, conversation and discussion to which they were intended to be conducive.

Bandello's *novelle* became available in French at about the same time as Marguerite's stories. By the late 1550s, however, the boisterous vitality of the early Renaissance, of which the flowering of the realistic short story had been a signal manifestation, was fast fading under the impact of a new yearning for orderliness and conformity. This was a trend of general import. In the field of aesthetics and creative writing it was represented by the rapid growth of classical poetics, largely under the influence of an Italian scholar, Julius Caesar Scaliger (1484-1558), who, we note, had settled as a physician at Agen at the time Bandello was acting bishop there; Scaliger's *Poetices Libri VII* was largely responsible for spreading Aristotle's theory of the dramatic unities in the dogmatic form that was to prevail in French seventeenth-century tragedy. The 1550s were also the period when Joachim du Bellay (1522-60), Pierre de Ronsard (1524-85) and the other *Pléiade* poets were restoring lyrical genres inherited from Greek and Latin antiquity and laying down strict rules for French versification, while Etienne Jodelle (1532-73) was producing the first classical tragedy in French. In the field of religion, the austerely rational ethics preached by Calvin (1509-64) was attracting many of the best minds in Protestant milieux to an exacting moral code that contrasted favourably with what was felt to be an undisciplined, individualistic laxity in the ebullience of Lutheran doctrine. At the same time, the Council of Trent (1545-63) was initiating a successful reform of the Roman church, whose dogmatic authority was consequently restored over a large part of Europe.

François de Belleforest (1530-84), the man who was chiefly responsible for adapting *Novella 44* and several other Bandello stories in his highly popular and often reprinted *Histoires tragiques* (1559), belonged to the new generation. He was bent on playing his part in the restoration of morality by making emphatically explicit such edifying potentialities as were latent in the Italian original. His purpose, he claimed, was not to titillate the sensuality of youthful French readers, but to guide them towards a sound assessment of good and evil:

> J'ay basti ces discours non pour chatoüiller les desirs à suyvre les inclinations du sensuel, mais à fin que la jeunesse Françoise, comme elle a l'esprit gentil et bon, voye et juge de la bonté et du vice.[4]

More specifically, some of the stories, he declared, were selected for translation because they were apt to generate disgust for sex: "à fin de faire savourer le desgoust qui est en ceste viande si peu plaisante." For Bandello, the edifying conclusion to the Ferrarese story was intended to give some respectability to an otherwise prurient narrative. To Belleforest, the tale was the attractive coating that would lure the reader into swallowing an austere message. To this end he contented himself with a terse summary of the original passage describing Parisina's almost heroic refusal to recant her lawless passion, and he eloquently expanded the uplifting report of Ugo's conversion and repentance. Moreover, Belleforest managed to shift the focus of the whole tale from the lovers to the Marquis: for Bandello's brief announcement of Niccolò's third marriage, he substituted his personal interpretation to the effect that the cruel murder of son and wife was in fact the punishment inflicted on Niccolò's persistent debauchery by God, who, "attendant la conversion du pécheur et le voyant endurcy en sa méchanceté, à la fin il le punit si aigrement que les générations suivantes se ressentent le plus souvent de la gravité de la punition". The French version thus brings him within the scope of a puritanical reprobation for any kind of sexual misdemeanour — a revealing instance of the way Western Christianity, whether in the form of Calvinistic puritanism or Tridentine authoritarianism, was trying to resume control of public morality in the middle of the sixteenth century.[5] Belleforest could not but reject Bandello's debonair toleration of sexual indulgence in men that was implicit in the honour code. At the end of the original tale he appended the uplifting information that the descendants of the Marquis would be punished for his misdeeds.

---

[4] For this and the following quotations, see Sturel, 52, 53 and 97.

[5] Despite his display of virtuous intentions, Belleforest was not spared posthumous criticism: in the middle of the next century another mediocre author of edifying fiction, Jean-Pierre Camus (1562-1653), who was a bishop as Bandello had been and a disciple of Saint François de Sales, complained that Belleforest's stories were "trop chargées de chair et de sang" (Sturel, 53).

In their minor way Bandello's tale and its French avatar manifest the growing application of a third principle of valuation to the situation of ethical transgression that I have called the Phaedra syndrome. Alongside the archaic fear of dishonour and shame, and the Stoic call to the inner voice of rational conscience, obedience to the will of God as codified by the Church was trying to recover the power it had wielded in medieval thinking: punishment and reward were no longer of a physical or social order, for they were raised to a "metaphysical" level. The sanction for infringing God's commandments was the spiritual soul's eternal damnation. Despite their potential significance as an index to changing mentalities,[6] these variations on the anecdotal story of Niccolò d'Este did not receive much learned attention until 1890, when the German scholar Adolf Schaeffer discovered that *Novella 44* was the ultimate source of one of Lope de Vega's masterpieces, *El castigo sin venganza* (I, 88). In 1928, however, Adolfo van Dam pointed out that Lope's *comedia* contained elements which had been introduced by Belleforest (59); it is not likely that the Spanish playwright had actually read Belleforest, for French had not yet achieved the status of the European elite's *lingua franca* it was to enjoy after Louis XIV. But van Dam's research revealed that a Spanish translation of various French stories of the time had been printed in Valladolid in 1603 as *Historicas tragicas exemplares*. As reprinted by van Dam in his edition of Lope's play, the Ferrarese story appears to be a rather indifferent translation of the Belleforest version. The Spanish author introduced two alterations that deserve mentioning: the Spanish title, "Historia de la Marquesa de Ferrara", refocuses

---

[6] Like Boccaccio's stories, Bandello's were chiefly designed for entertainment. It has long been assumed that this was also how the French audience of the time appraised their many translations and imitations. In 1903, it was Gustave Reynier's hypothesis that "il semble que les lecteurs aient été assez insensibles à cette intention moralisatrice et qu'ils aient surtout cherché dans les *Histoires tragiques* ce que le titre promettait, c'est-à-dire des péripéties violentes et des dénouements brutaux" (164). More recently, however, Donald Stone demonstrated the enormous popularity of Belleforest's collection as evidenced in many printings between 1559 and 1616 (Stone 1972); this, he claimed, was not solely due to their more questionable aspects, but chiefly to their educational value, which made them almost compulsory reading for the daughters of well-to-do families and the most learned among courtiers: in the words of Jacques Yver (1521-71), "aujourd'huy c'est une honte entre les filles bien nourries et entre les mieux apprins courtisans de les ignorer" (quoted by Stone 1973, 30-31).

the reader's attention on the female transgressor; more important, the text itself has been enriched with an even stronger dose of Christian commentary than Belleforest had instilled into Bandello's narrative.

The spirit of free investigation of the early Renaissance had made the kind of many-shaped moral transgression inherent in the Phaedra syndrome once more acceptable as subject-matter for creative artists. In the seventeenth century, the Christian outlook powerfully re-installed from the middle of the sixteenth was to appear as a fundamental element of ethical appraisal. In the person of Bandello's Marquis the shame-culture code of aristocratic honour and Christian morality were seen to be acting unreflectingly in peaceful coexistence. Whether this should be taken to imply that the Western mind had worked out a satisfactory, holistic synthesis of outward and inward sanctions and criteria is by no means self-evident.

4

JUSTICE AND REVENGE RECONCILED: LOPE DE VEGA'S *EL CASTIGO SIN VENGANZA* (1634)

In his study of Matteo Bandello's French translators and imitators Frank Hook perceptively remarked that "Bandello, like his predecessor, Boccaccio, had a good sense of narrative technique; his stories move rapidly, often to atone for a poverty of plot. Belleforest seems to have had a positive genius for destroying the narrative movement of a story" (11). It took the vision and craft of a Shakespeare or a Lope de Vega not only to restore movement and to create plot interest, but also to deepen the psychological analysis and to integrate ethical perspectives into the dramatic development of such tales. When Lope adapted Bandello's *Novella 44* into *El castigo sin venganza*, he obviously allocated far more attention to the plight of the Theseus-figure, the father-ruler, than had been the case previously.

His promoting the Italian marquis to ducal status can be accounted for by the fact that Ferrara had become a dukedom in the fifteenth century. Yet this was by no means what Menéndez Pidal described as an "insignificant change from a dramatic point of view" (128): it was part of Lope's strategy of magnifying the moral significance of the character, an intention which, as we shall see, is confirmed by other alterations in plot and psychology. There is much truth in A. David Kossof's observation (anticipated by Harri Meier, 243-46) to the effect that "the focus of interest is not the adulterous love between the young lovers but the relation between father and son" (31).

Actually, this *comedia* is an inordinately complex one in which no incident, no relational cluster is meaningless. In compliance with the higher preoccupations of the time, it is as much a theological play as Tirso de Molina's *El burlador de Sevilla*. In the person of the Duke of Ferrara, the Spanish playwright worked out a problem of major importance in Tridentine Europe: the problem raised by the possible contradiction between the Christian view of legitimate punishment (*castigo*) and the concept of private revenge enjoined by the aristocratic code of honour (*venganza*). This is thoroughly worked out in the final scenes. In compliance with the holistic baroque outlook, Lope found, in the Bandello story, a situation in which both elements could be syncretically reconciled; the Duke has his son executed — the death of his wife seems to be of little import to him or to anyone else — not in a spirit of hateful revenge, but *despite* his continued fatherly love; he legitimitaly inflicts deserved punishment in his capacity as God's magistrate in his dukedom; yet he does not kill the young man with his own hand and everything is effected in comparative secrecy. His worldly honour is thus restored as a consequence of his regard for Christian duty.

While the complexity of this many-faceted play must be kept in mind, much of the dramatic interest resides in the love affair between the son, here called Federico, and his stepmother, who is now ominously renamed Casandra. Since they are both guilty, the young pair should be regarded, in the present context, as jointly acting out the transgressive role that is Phaedra's in the classical tradition. Viewing the play from this angle, comparison should make it possible to determine Lope's own contribution to the development of the adultery-cum-incest motif in the aftermath of the Counter-Reformation.

In Bandello's story Parisina falls in love with Ugo while actively seeking sexual compensation for her husband's neglect of his marital duty (518); the young woman's assertion that she was in love with her stepson even before she met her husband (521-22) must thus be taken as a palpable lie that throws unfavourable light on her character almost from the outset. Lope turns this lie into truth: as Casandra is driving along a river from Mantua to her marriage in Ferrara, she has an accident and is nearly drowned. She is rescued by Count Federico, who is on his way to welcome her on behalf of his father. While this may be reminiscent of Tristan escorting his uncle Mark's bride, Yseult, to Cornwall, it should be noted that Federico sets out on his mission with unconcealed reluctance. The rescue incident is one of the symbolic devices frequently used in the Spanish *comedia*: an unobtrusive portent that Casandra will eventually drown in unrestrained sensuality.[1]

---

[1] The premonitory symbolism of such incidents in the plays of Lope de Vega and Calderón has been fruitfully analysed by Victor Nixon and Angel Valbuena-Briones among others.

For the moment, however, the impromptu meeting, coming just after the audience has witnessed the Duke's gross philandering, throws an aura of naturalness and innocence around two young people obviously suited to each other. Yet their verbal responses to the encounter are markedly different. The young woman insists that she is and will remain the Count's mother; she wants him to honour her by that name; her further statement that having him for her son gives her greater joy than becoming Duchess of Ferrara may be taken as a sample of aristocratic courtliness or as a mild suggestion of more than motherly interest. Federico is less subdued; he bursts into a firework display of extravagant conceits involving his soul, God, the sun, and the far-fetched *concetto* that he is truly the first son his father expects from his new wife since he has just been born again (498-526). This orgy of figurative language may be the spontaneous overflow of powerful feelings. We must recall, however, that the play opened with the Duke's brief, seemingly irrelevant indictment of the foolish ramblings (*desatinos*, 12) of a "new sect" (19) of hacks who have reduced poetry to such a "miserable state" that it has become a brainless playing with many-coloured ribbons (25-32), for which Lope coins the unflattering epithet *cultidiablesco* (53). Federico's far-fetched style may well be a parodic example of the new-fangled *culteranisto* taste for obscure, elaborate ornamentation. Lope possibly designed his speech in such a way as to convey a sense of artificial literariness or orotund self-delusion.[2]

The notion that a match between Casandra and Federico would be more natural and apposite than the impending marriage is first explicitly formulated by their servants, Lucrecia (588-90) and Batín (638-39). These are their masters' confidants. Unlike Phaedra's Nurse, they play no active part in the development of the plot. They display understanding, at times compassion, but their main function is theatrical: it is to allow their masters to vent their feelings for the benefit of the audience.

---

[2] Harry W. Hilborn correctly points out that Lope, despite his antagonism to *culteranismo*, allowed himself in *El castigo sin venganza* to "succumbir a la moda gongorina de su tiempo"; he quotes several passages that were indeed obviously written "sin sugestión de censura ni mofa". In the case of Federico, however, the character's subsequent development will demonstrate that his ornate speeches function as a lofty disguise for the shallowness of his feelings and the intensity of his carnal appetites.

By the end of Act I the protagonists' reactions to their servants' innuendos has shown the extent of Lope's independence from Bandello: both Casandra and Federico appear to be resigned and determined to resist the call of love. Different motives account for such restraint. Despite Casandra's awareness of her prospective husband's "free living" (604-605), she will go on to Ferrara and an unattractive match: she cannot change her misguided fate and marry Federico, for her father would kill her if she were to return to Mantua; and even if he did not, she argues in terms redolent of Phaedra's concern with her reputation in Euripides (*Hipp* 692), her folly would be the fable of all Italy ("por toda Italia fuera/fábula mi desatino", 596-98).

More attention is given to the tormented mood of Federico, to whom Lope has awarded a bride, the Duke's wealthy niece, Aurora. The two cousins have grown up together since infancy in loving harmony (712-32); yet the Count does not so much as mention her when he laments his fate to Batín at the close of the first Act. In a revised version of the antinomy between *furor* and *ratio* in Seneca's *Phaedra*, he bewails the irrational frenzy generated by his imagination:

> cosas imagina un hombre
> que al más abrasado enfermo
> con frenesí no pudieran
> llegar a su entendimiento.
> (932-35)

Unlike his model in Bandello he displays his religious sense at this early stage, beseeching Jesus and God to protect him against the "mad notions of his waking dreams":

> ¡Jesús! ¡Dios me valga! ¡Afuera,
> desatinatos conceptos
> de sueños despiertos!
> (958-60)

He curses his "egregious folly" ("extraña locura", 964), but when Batín invites him to disclose his secret, he replies that he is not trying to conceal anything, since his imaginings are mere bodiless spirits ("que las imaginaciones/son espíritus sin cuerpo", 968-69). And as soon as Batín has uttered his correct guess — "your stepmother" (978) — he silences him, adding however — in lame self-defence that calls to mind Phaedra's "mei non sum potens" and "quid ratio possit?" — that he cannot be held guilty since he has no control over his thoughts: "... yo,/¿qué culpa tengo,/pues el pensamiento es libre?" (981-82).

Lope shaped the shallow characters he inherited from Bandello with truly admirable psychological insight and artistic skill. Throughout the first Act Casandra is presented as a matter-of-fact young person, who accepts her fate, albeit by no means whole-heartedly, out of fear of the external sanctions (her father's wrath, public ridicule) that refusing the *mariage de convenance* at this stage would entail. In her eyes the emerging problem is solved as soon as she realizes that her lovable rescuer is her stepson to be. She can hardly have any sense of guilt for she can entertain no deep feelings towards her middle-aged libertine fiancé; nor does she contemplate indulging in any objectionable deed. The episode by the river's bank simply marks the end of a pleasant beginning.

In all this she is starkly different from Federico, whose disturbed mood finds suitable expression in the jerky exclamatory style of his conversation with Batín. Although he may seek ethical relief of a sort in the notion that he is not responsible for the phantasms of his imagination, his sense of propriety is dismayed by mental images that obscenely violate the proper relationship between father and son. The unthinkable, which fills him with incredulous horror, is his envying his father's luck: "Con ser imposible, llego/a estar envidioso dél" (987-88). Like Hippolytus in the old tale, he recoils from the thought of incest. But being in love with Casandra, he also has the instinctive reaction of Euripides' Phaidra: the stain in his heart must remain undivulged (*Hipp* 317), and silence and concealment are the best way of handling the situation (*Hipp* 393), which is why he enjoins silence on his servant-confidant, "no le digas" (980). And, true to the Phaedra model, he concludes with a death-wish:

> Con eso puedo
> morir de imposible amor,
> y tener posibles celos.
> (991-93)

The contrast in Casandra's and Federico's early response to their brief encounter is confirmed in the first half of the second Act. A whole month has elapsed. Casandra has experienced the Duke's scornful neglect; but although she forcefully expresses her resentment to Lucrecia (996-1072), she gives no hint that a love affair might develop between her and her stepson. Indeed the text offers no reason for presuming that her feelings are other than motherly. She is genuinely concerned lest Federico might fear to lose part of his inheritance to the children she might bear the Duke. And in the greater part of the decisive dialogue with Federico that occupies the central section of play (1319-1453), she will sincerely attempt to reconcile him with Aurora.

As to Federico, after a month of allegedly unbearable frustration and remorse, he is still not dead. His inner despondency takes the outward form of a melancholy that is almost ostentatious: it strikes everyone at court and even causes his father to consult the doctors of Ferrara and Mantua (1125). The death-wish has not left him. It is now reiterated in front of Batín in convoluted language:

> Y si muriera, quisieria
> poder volver a vivir
> mil veces, para morir
> cuantas a vivir volviera...
> (1204-1207)

> (If I should die, I wish
> I could return to live a thousand times,
> for I should wish to have
> as many deaths as lives...)

In its alliterative way, such "poetic" jabber is in line with the young man's *culteranista* expostulation to Casandra in Act I; but dubious light is cast on his over-refined word play by the ironic element of parody in Batín's reply, which derides both the style and substance of his master's words:

> Segun eso, ni tú quieres
> vivir, Conde, ni morir,
> que entre morir y vivir
> como hermafrodita eres,
> que como aquél se compone
> de hombre y mujer, tú de muerte
> y vida.
> (1216-1222)

> (It seems, sir, that you want
> neither to live nor to die.
> Between living and dying
> you are like a hermaphrodite:
> you hesitate between death and life
> as he does between male and female.)

The pastiche enhances the antithesis between Federico's affected style and Casandra's matter-of-factness. It throws retrospective suspicion on the trustworthiness of the young man's flowery language when he first met his father's bride, and also, perhaps, on the real depth of the sense of guilt so pathetically conveyed at the end of Act I. At any rate it should invite audience and reader to reconsider their assessment of Count Federico's personality and of the nature of his love.

The quality of the young man's passion is usually taken at its face-value. Harri Meier seems to have reflected the general view, albeit with unusual enthusiasm, when he claimed that "O amor de Federico já não é a sensualidade dos protagonistas esfomeados o doentes de amor que nos oferecem a novela e o drama renascentistas, é, pelo contrário, um sentido metafísico da vida, uma aspiração espiritualizada do sentido da perfeição da alma, uma força que impulsiona o coração generoso para o belo e para o nobre" (243-44). Close reading of the text in its context makes such uncritical acquiescence in the Count's own self-projected image untenable. William C. McCrary analysed the *comedia* in terms of role-playing, a concept that should prove fruitful within proper limits. A case can be made for the notion that Batín's mild mockery suggests that Federico is just producing more rhetorical gems of the kind that had adorned his first address to Casandra, though now applied to a different topic. To the *gracioso*'s wry commonsense, Federico's elegant ravings are but bloated bathos. Nevertheless their content can hardly be described as a feigned death-wish designed to influence other persons as it was on the lips of Seneca's Phaedra. Indeed, Federico rounds off his declamation with a tell-tale piece of clever sophistry: if he refrains from committing suicide, that is because death would be less painful than staying alive (1212-15).

Youthful infatuation mistaken for deep passion, genuine remorse turning into rhetorical exercises: this is the key to Federico's fickle personality. His true concern is to produce the verbal response expected of any courtly hero of refined literary culture under such interesting circumstances. As to the nature of his *imposible amor*, there is nothing "metaphysical" or "spiritual" about it: the horrifying image that occasioned his genuine sense of guilt at the end of Act I, perhaps the only moment of real self-revelation in his stage career, was generated by the ugly image of himself taking the wife of his revered father to bed. It is this carnal element that will take control and lead to his undoing.

The character of Casandra has likewise been interpreted in a variety of contradictory ways. Clearly her model in Bandello is a straightforward illustration of the phallocratic tradition that woman's frailty is ultimately responsible for the sins and sufferings of mankind. Lope's version, however, is far more subtle and complex. It creates a polysemic conundrum for experts to exercise their wits on. In 1948, Harri Meier confidently asserted that "No encontro de Federico com Cassandra criou Lope uma psicologia dos sexos típica para o classicismo espanhol. Cassandra é tudo menos sensual, falta de escrúpulos, irreflectida" (244). Four decades later McCrary argued that "It is vital to an appreciation of Lope's plan in this act to grasp that it is Federico's artful play-acting that leads Casandra to the truth", that is, to acknowledge her sexual attraction to the Count, hitherto hidden behind the "absurd pose" of her "understanding mother act" (212-13). Yet to dismiss her role-playing in the first part of Act II as "absurd" is to gloss over the element of naive conscientiousness in this young woman's make-up. In her commonsensical way she has forgotten (or inhibited, or repressed) the attraction she had briefly admitted to Lucrecia in line 591. Even the servant's reiteration that it would have been more natural and reasonable ("conforme a naturaleza y a la razón") for her to have married the Count (1097-1103) fails to elicit any response. Here and throughout the first part of the fateful dialogue with Federico (1319-1478), her mind is wholly absorbed by the sorrow and resentment due to her husband's shameless philandering. There is a faint element of threat in her comment that the Duke should fear lest his disgraceful behaviour might arouse lawless thoughts in her mind (1070-73). Although the threat is soon repeated more pointedly (1136-37), there is no intimation that the idea of using her stepson as an instrument for deserved reprisal against her lewd husband has obtruded itself upon her. Her attractive combination of kindliness and practical sense makes it credible that she is sincere when she tries to help Aurora — like herself a victim of male inconstancy.

Casandra's words and actions provide no evidence that prospects of an affair with Federico may be lurking at the back of her mind until the dialogue with the young man that exactly occupies the middle section of the play. Her purpose in initiating this interview is to reassure Federico on two points: he has no reason for being jealous of the relationship between Aurora and the Marquis of Gonzaga, who escorted her from Mantua; and he has no reason to fear that she will bear the Duke a legitimate heir. The young man dispels her misgivings on both counts, but he confesses that his melancholy springs from an unhappy love which is not directed at his cousin. This leads in a very natural way to

Casandra's question, "Who is she?" (1442), prompting the Count's telltale reply that he aims higher: "Más alto/vuela el pensamiento mío" (1445-46). From this point on, Aurora's name, revealingly, is no longer mentioned. Casandra, who had just expressed astonishment that Aurora should disdain such a noble knight as Federico, "discreto, dulce y tan digno/de ser querido" (1438-39), now shifts to a level of ambiguous generality: how could "any woman" informed of his love fail to love him in return? (1447-50). It is likely — and performance can make this clear — that the prospect of a different kind of relationship with her stepson is dawning in her mind now that her imagination has been spurred by her recent recital of her husband's misdemeanours as much as by the thought of the Count's qualities that she has just extolled on behalf of Aurora.

In his tantalizingly inconclusive reply ("If you knew ...", 1453-54) the Count expatiates on the folly ("locura", 1478) of his "impossible" passion, calling in true *cultodiablesca* manner on an impressive array of classical allusions to Phaeton, Icarus, Bellerophon, the Trojan War and Jason. Throughout this display of erudition his better mind is still in control and he does not let out that the object of his passion is Casandra herself. There is mild irony in the Duchess's seemingly impersonal retort. In a detached, amused way, she reminds him that women are not made of bronze or alabaster and she gives him a recipe for conquering his beloved, "whoever she may be" ("sea quien fuera", 1490). In dictating what he should say, she even borrows his own ornate style, summoning Venus, Diana and Endymion before she concludes, quite matter-of-factly, that "even the most chaste mansion has a door made of wax: speak your love, do not die in silence" (1499-1501).

In order to express how sorely tempted he finds himself, the Count resorts to a less erudite animal story, the Pelican fable, whose meaning he clarifies as follows: "my thoughts, the children of my love, are being consumed with fire" (1514-17). He is almost carried away by the explosive mixture of passion and fear that boils in his mind, and he apostrophizes his stepmother directly in short, vehement sentences that convey the dread irony of his predicament: he understands Casandra's advice to mean that he should declare his love *for her*, and this gives unprecedented intensity to the realization — not that "his love is foolish" as Mitchell D. Triwedi would have it (329) — but that disclosure is so dangerous ("porque es tanto mi peligro") that he had better reverse the Duchess's advice and "die in silence" (1528-31). As he exits with his secret still technically undivulged, it is difficult to agree with MacCrary's view that his "rhetoric indicates that he has now cast himself, at least in his mind's eye, in the role of the distant courtly lover smitten with a forbidden passion" (212). This may be an apposite comment to the would-be dazzling display of classical learning in lines 1453-76, but the changing stylistic mode in the Pelican fable and in the ensuing apostrophes betrays the shift in his mood. Though the iterative death-wish at the end is still part of Fernando's emotional orating, he is genuinely frightened at the thought that he might be drawn into a real-life affair with his father's attractive wife.

Casandra's soliloquy between this dialogue and the announcement of the Duke's departure is of decisive importance and deserves minute attention. Here, in the stylized manner proper to the *comedia*, Lope provides the audience with the key to the Duchess's view of her own problem, now that Federico has virtually declared his love. Although she describes her confused state of mind in almost cosmic terms (1532-51), she defines the issues at stake clearly enough. She ascribes her confusion to the seductive but deceitful workings of her imagination. It is her imagination that tells her that the Count is in love with her (1552-53); the same imagination tells her that such love is impossible (1554-55) — presumably because it involves adultery and incest. As she recalls her unhappy marriage, she acquiesces in what she "feels" ("en lo que siento consiento", 1558); and what she "feels", what is uppermost in her mind, is a yearning to take revenge upon her "barbarous husband" (1564). Her imagination tricks her into fancying that what is impossible can easily be accomplished (1565-66). It is the awareness of such manifold contradictions that makes her crazy ("que me enloquecen", 1565). At the same time as she imagines herself avenged, she recalls that adultery is a lawless crime ("error tan injusto", 1569) and she sees the Duke's sword cast its shadow on her desire (1570-71).

At no point in this soliloquy do we find any intimation that "love" for the Count might be a significant element in the temptation to which she is subjected. When she stops delving in her confusion to examine what she should actually do, she acknowledges that despite the Count's sterling qualities it would be folly for her to open the door to such mad passion, meaning of course *his* passion (1573-75). She therefore decides to overcome her "stupid confusion" (1576) and implores heaven to help her:

>   Salid, cielo, a la defensa,
>   aunque no yerra quien piensa,
>   porque en el mundo no hibiera
>   hombre con honra si fuera
>   ofensa pensar la ofensa.
>   Hasta agora no han errado
>   ni mi honor, ni mi sentido,
>   porque lo que he consentido
>   ha sido un error pintado.
>   Consentir lo imaginado,
>   para con Dios es error,
>   ma no para el deshonor;
>   que diferencian intentos
>   el ver Dios los pensamientos
>   y no los ver el honor.
>   (1577-1591)
>
> (Come, heaven to my defence,
> although to think is not to err,
> for if the thought of an offence could give offence,
> no man on earth would have preserved his honour.
> So far, neither my honour nor my judgment have erred
> for I have only consented to a painted error.
> To consent to one's imaginings is sinful in the eyes of God,
> but not in the eyes of honour.
> Intentions are different.
> God knows our thoughts,
> but honour knows them not.)

These terse statements disentangle the interplay of three aspects of ethical behaviour — involuntary thoughts, mental acquiescence in lawless thoughts, actual misdeeds — and of the two basic codes of her society: the demands of honour and the prescriptions of Christian morality. Like Federico (see 981-82), Casandra exonerates herself of any guilt for her involuntary thoughts. That her mind dwelt willingly on the idea of taking revenge upon her husband is no crime either, whether against her honour (1583) or against the Duke's: if it were an offence to think of an offence, there is no man in the world but would have his honour wronged (1578-81), and what she has consented to is just the mental picture of a misdeed (1584-85), not an actual one. And while mental acquiescence is a crime in the eyes of God, who sees all our thoughts, it does not infringe the honour code.

There are two conceivable reasons why Casandra should request God's help. One is to refrain from translating her vengeful lust into a deed that would destroy both her honour and the Duke's, and thus constrain the latter to take vengeance upon her. The other, presumably, is to repress, if not her uncontrollable imaginings, at least her sinful conscious entertaining of them. Whatever may have been in her (and Lope's) mind, what follows demonstrates that her prayer is not granted. Furthermore, her part in the ensuing course of the action throws ambiguous light on the concluding lines of this stock-taking soliloquy. It is somewhat surprising that her carefully constructed speech does not end on what would have been a suitable climax, the fear of divine omniscience, but on the almost relieved observation that honour is not concerned with undivulged thoughts. It does not seem idle to speculate that Lope may have intended this to point to Casandra's *hamartia*: what really matters to her is not God's judgment, but her husband's honour; what truly preoccupies her is not the inwardness of virtue but impunity from outward sanctions.

This is bound to alter our appraisal of her personality. Until this moment ("hasta agora", 1582), she has been presented in a constantly favourable light as an unhappy bride who, as van Dam put it, "ha de captar forzosamente nuestra simpatía" (1928, 104). But her now wobbling scale of values should help audience and reader to grasp the change that is taking place. Not inadvertently did the playwright append to this soliloquy a very brief but revealing scene, in which Casandra's personality takes on an uncontrovertibly negative colouring: as Aurora anxiously inquires after the results of the conversation with the Count, the poker-faced Duchess utters a shameless lie, assuring Aurora that Federico is still in love with her. From now on van Dam's roseate assessment of Casandra's character loses much of its relevance and must be superseded by the often intense dislike it has earned from a number of recent critics.[3] There is in her a strain of dishonesty that will take the upper hand as soon as an occasion arises.

This occasion is the husband-father-ruler's departure. Here again Lope has significantly altered his data: the Duke is not — as in the Bandello-Belleforest version — called to Milan on some unspecified feudal business: he is summoned to Rome by the Pope in order to head the army of the Church against its enemies in Italy (1682-95). The new situation opens unforeseen vistas for the young pair. Federico's

---

[3] T.E. May's unfavourable assessment was later condoned by Geraldine Nichols.

response is one of bewilderment, which he lyrically summarizes in a sonnet (1797-1880) that culminates in a proclamation of self-denial: all things are possible for a true lover, he claims, except this incestuous passion which must be denied gratification for ever. Contrariwise, Casandra's ensuing soliloquy (1811-55) shows her, as Victor Dixon aptly notes, "significantly further advanced along the road to sin" (74).

The sexual element *now for the first time* obtrudes itself as she dreams of mingling pleasure with revenge (1824). At this stage she appears almost as an exact replica of Seneca's Phaedra: she is conscious that the design which is rapidly taking shape in her mind is dishonourable (1814), evil (1822), mad (1823-25) and sinful (1854). At the same time, like Phaedra, she seeks justification in her husband's disgraceful conduct (1822), in the Count's noble character (1826) and even in the example set by the many women who betrayed their husbands or fell in love with their fathers or brothers — which prompts her to argue that no incest is envisaged since Federico is not related to her by blood (1850). Despite this balanced assessment of pros and cons, Casandra's lust for revenge, now joined to sexual lust and encouraged by the Duke's impending absence, proves more powerful than her moral scruples and rational fears. When she sees Federico, she crowns her soliloquy with a brief utterance that echoes Phaedra's "Aude, anima" (503): "I am determined. What do I fear?" (1856-57).

This ushers in the great temptation scene that seals their tragic fate. With unwonted astuteness Casandra first appeals to the Count's *culto* taste for classical erudition. In order to alleviate his love-sickness (the object of which she is still supposed not to know with certainty) she recounts the parallel story of Antiochus,[4] thus beguiling him into making a clean breast. At this point the dialogue gives way to a sort of duet in which both lovers intone the same elegiac theme, albeit with

---

[4] According to Plutarch, the Syrian prince Antiochus (325-261 BC) fell in love with Stratonice, second wife of his father, King Seleucus. He tried so hard to repress this passion that he fell seriously ill. When informed by his physician of the cause of the young man's disease, the magnanimous monarch turned her over to his son (Demetrius, 38). The story became popular during the Renaissance thanks to the Plutarch translations by Amyot in French (1559) and North in English (1579) and to its inclusion in William Painter's collection, *The Palace of Pleasure* (1566-67). It inspired several minor French playwrights in the seventeenth century. In Spain it was to be handled by Agustín Moreto (1618-69) in *Antíoco y Seleuco*, whose structure, as has often been noted, owed much to *El castigo sin venganza*.

significant variations. Their common frame of reference is defined by parameters that have by now become familiar: such a love affair would offend both God and the Duke; love and death are therefore inextricably intertwined: eternal life is threatened as well as physical survival. For Federico this is a moment of lyrical intensity highlighted by the *concetto* that he now finds himself "sin mí, sin vos y sin Dios" because his passion is contrary to God's law, because he cannot possess the woman he loves and because he has lost his soul to her. This tormenting sense of dispossession amounts to a poetic amplification of the death-wish. Reader and audience cannot but be filled with pity and sympathy for this desperate young man. The problem, however, is not whether he is sincere. Although it would be unwise to assert that Federico does not mean what he says, we may, and indeed should, wonder whether (in Donald Larson's phrasing) he has not become "entrapped in his own courtly rhetoric" (138): Larson perceptively observed that "when Federico first speaks of dying (1212-15), it is still with a fairly strong sense of attachment to life" (136), but this attachment becomes increasingly "attenuated" as the play goes on. It will be part of the function of Act III to enlighten us on this point.

As to Casandra, starting from the same recognition of transgression, she cleverly blows hot and cold, effectively fanning Federico's flame: their love is bound to be severely punished by the Duke and by God; yet many have erred before; the only remedy — "Si remedio puede haber" (1991), recalling Phaedra's "unicum effugium mali" (253) — is to stop seeing each other. Whereas Federico has just claimed that he had rather die than remain enslaved to his guilty passion (1926-30), Casandra manages to twist the logical conclusion of her own argument into what is in effect an undisguised declaration of love:

> Huye de mí, que de ti
> yo no sé si huir podré,
> o me mataré por ti.
> (1996-98)
>
> (Leave me, for I do not know
> whether I shall be able to leave you,
> or shall kill myself for you.)

The whole of this final scene of Act II is a masterpiece of ambivalence and equivocation unparalleled in Western drama. While the two lovers prepare to leave the stage by opposite exits, Federico's requesting and obtaining permission to touch Casandra's hand is a symbolic gesture of contained sensuousness showing that they are now united in mutual passion. The antinomy between this and their words brings out the dialectics of love and death: although they are aware of the unavoidable consequences of decisions that have not yet been clearly formulated, they are now powerless to resist their emotional impulses. Lope's artistry has created a poetic-theatrical equivalent of Seneca's "Mei non sum potens". But the sense of fatality that oozes from the behaviour and the discourse of the two lovers should not be mistaken for fatalism in Lope, who has been at pains at each stage in the development of the dramatic action to display his characters' vivid awareness of the correct way to eschew sin and its attendant perils.

Their *hamartía* does not reside in flawed intellect — as is the case with Euripides' Phaidra, or with Othello — but in a failure of the will, as in Seneca's Phaedra, or in Macbeth. Neither of them has been able to muster enough will-power to do what either knew to be right. Federico should have kept to his early insight that his infatuation must be repressed; Casandra should have taken Lucrecia's hint to seek her father's protection against her husband's faithlessness (1094-95). Post-Romantic sentimental prejudices have prevented many commentators of the play from realizing that no one in Catholic Golden Age Spain could possibly miss the point: the Count and the Duchess are definitely not innocent, pitiable, star-crossed lovers of the Romeo-and-Juliet variety; they are, and should be held, responsible for their lawless liaison.

In *El castigo sin venganza* as in other Lope *comedias*, it is the function of the final Act to clarify the issues and to dispel such misconceptions as the playwright himself has artfully induced in the minds of readers and audience. There is no overt moralizing in the original Italian tale, although the separate paths followed by the young lovers once they are imprisoned was probably Bandello's contrived manner of illustrating the difference between obduracy in evil (Parisina) and contrition leading to spiritual salvation (Ugo). Belleforest had found it necessary to add some more explicit sermonizing of his own. In the Spanish translation discovered by van Dam and probably used by Lope, this reads as follows:

> Lo que de aqui se puede colegir es que se deue considerar lo que se comiença, y lo que se puede seguir dello, antes de ponerlo en execución. Y se entendera que si el pecado se arrayga, echa sus rayzes tan adentro, que son

trabajosas de arrancar. Es este marauilloso exemplo para los que viuen sin tener cuenta con lo que ordenan la carne y el demonio.

(82)

(What one may conclude from this is that one should consider well what one is beginning, and the consequences that may follow from it, before putting it into effect. For anyone can understand that if sin takes hold, it throws its roots so deep that they are difficult to pull out. This example is an excellent one for those who live without taking into account the power of the flesh and the devil [trans. Larson, 132]).

It goes without saying that this kind of bottom-rung oratory could not suit Lope's purposes, whatever they were. If the lovers' punishment was to be presented as lawful and consonant with both the honour code and Christian morality, it was necessary to raise the ethical status of Bandello's Ferrarese potentate: hence the alteration in the assignment that accounts for his absence from court; hence also his conversion after kissing the Pope's hand (2316-27); hence, too, his insistent need to reassure himself that the death penalty inflicted on his son and his wife is not a wilful act of private vengeance (2546-47, 2834-48). To this sudden reversal in the personality of the Duke corresponds an equally startling change in the image projected by the lovers. In this respect Lope departed from the Bandello model in two highly significant ways.

First, he gave them time to react to the news of the Duke's return, just in the same way and for the same reason Seneca (to be followed by Racine) allowed Phaidra to outlive Hippolytus. This made it possible to have them reveal, under stress though in circumstances that they have been anticipating from the outset, a new facet of their characters. Hardly has Federico been informed of his father's impending arrival that he abruptly starts courting Aurora, feigning jealousy towards the Marquis Gonzaga (2161-64). Although he tells Batín that he is so disturbed he does not know what he is doing, his true intent will soon be unveiled. As Casandra arrives, the elegiac death theme recurs, for the last time on their lips: since they cannot live without "seeing" each other as they have become used to, the only issue is to die (2257-68). This however is merely the conventional language of literary courtliness. The Duchess's insistant questioning (2265, 2266, 2269) suggests that instead of heroically accepting the fatal death for which we have been led to think they were preparing, she hopes that her lover will come forward with some nice little scheme enabling them to stay alive and enjoy each other. And so he does: "From now on, I shall feign to woo and love Aurora. I shall even ask her in marriage from the Duke"

(2270-73), so that the latter will have no suspicion and disregard palace rumours.

To the audience this should come as a stunning revelation: this personable young nobleman, this unhappy victim of a sinful, impossible passion, who never tired of rehearsing his eagerness to die, this erudite poetic *cultista* now discloses himself to be a lewd scheming knave who is desperately planning to have it both ways: he now proposes to marry honest Aurora in order to keep his mistress and to further deceive his loving father. This is the reader's disillusioned *anagnorisis*, a breathtaking moment of *desengaño*, when the painted veil of appearances is lifted to expose the unpalatable reality: lust in action in a waste of shame. Nor is this all. Although the Count's hypocritical courting was contemptuously snubbed by Aurora (2182-204), he does take his unholy marriage proposal to the Duke (2557-74) in brainless disregard of what his alleged bride's response is likely to be. At the same time and for good measure, he seizes this occasion to insert slanderous innuendoes about the Duchess who, he claims, "although she was an angel to all has not been so to me" (2597-98) and "at times loved to show me that those who are born of other women cannot be treated as sons" (2604-605).

Federico's conduct throughout is all the more erratically irrational as he appears to overlook that his scheming will also be countered by Casandra, whose reaction was, to say the least, definitely negative:

¡Agravios! no bastan celos?
¿Casarte? Estás, Conde en ti?
(2276-77)

What the contemplated marriage arouses in her is more than love jealousy (*celos*): she resents it as an offence (*agravios*), an unbearable insult to her pride. She is so incensed that she starts reviling him as a wicked traitor, who was responsible for their quandary in the first place (2280-85). A veritable shrew now, she scolds him and shouts at him that she had rather be killed a thousand times by her husband than see her lover marry Aurora. But when she meets the Duke after regaining her composure, she has found a more astute way to obstruct the Count's self-seeking project: immediately after Federico has informed his father of his wish to marry Aurora, the Duchess in her turn asks the Duke to allow Aurora to marry the Marquis Gonzaga (2662-64). In predictable surprise the Duke tells her of his son's own request, which leads Casandra to conclude, in a dejected aside, that "the treacherous count has tired of me" (2696-97). But this rekindles her wrath and when the Count appears, she resumes her shouting, calling him "traitor", "villain", "low-born coward" and even, climactically, "dog" (2699-730). Her foul language is as revealing of the darker side of her personality as was Federico's underhand device. Her character does not exhibit the same kind of contradiction as does Federico's: in hindsight, her resentment at her husband's neglect is seen to have been due less to unrequited love or even sexual frustration than to wounded pride. She finds herself abandoned for the second time: this is more than her self-love can bear; she no longer controls herself; uglier potentialities in her make-up are allowed to come to the surface.

At this final stage Federico has relinquished his inflated, melancholy babble, which can now be seen to have been no more than a mask of self-delusion. As he frankly explains in order to pacify, or at least silence, his irate mistress, his sole preoccupation is to preserve, as he attentionately puts it, "our" lives ("asegurar/nuestra vida", 2721-22). The marriage scheme, he claims, was mere pretence aimed at the Duke — who is eavesdropping the while. After weathering a last salvo of insults (2730-37), he solemnly gives Casandra his word that he will do anything she wishes, advising her to feign pleasure in her husband's company. The woman's response (the last words she has occasion to utter) is exceedingly ambiguous:

> Pues no hay amor imposible.
> Tuya he sido y tuya estoy;
> no ha de faltar invención
> para vernos cada día
> . . . .
>   Así lo haré
> sin tu ofensa; que yo sé
> que el que es fingido no es gusto
>   (2766-775)
>
> (There is no impossible love, then.
> I have been yours and still am yours;
> we shall not lack devices to meet every day ...
> I will do as you say;
> this will be no offence to you,
> for I know that feigned pleasure is not pleasure.)

She has just inveighed against the falsity of men (2761). Does she now really believe him? Or is she pretending to agree in his new scheme? Much will depend on the actress who plays the role. Nor does it matter much: whether she is truly willing to follow his advice and betray the Duke in more subtly impudent ways, or feigns to believe him while secretly preparing some other scheme of her own, the fact remains that they are now united in dissembling and betrayal.

It was in order to make this point that Lope boldly inserted the first part of Act III into the Bandello plot. The contrast between Parisina and Ugo in their preparation for death was too crudely obvious for his genius. He wanted this story, which Batín reports had struck Italy with amazement and fear, to be an example (*ejemplo*, 3201) for Spain, but he did not wish it to display the stilted didacticism of the medieval *exemplum*. The message was to be conveyed through rounded characters that could be perceived to change under stress, thus unveiling the dark reality of their deeper selves, originally hidden behind the touching mask of courtly love and tragic rhetoric.

Lope's other departure from the source *dénouement*, the manner of the lovers' death, has often been noted. Amado Alonso very plausibly argued that the Duke, unlike his model in Bandello, had to have both lovers killed without warning because the Spanish code of honour required the execution to be performed secretly (10) whereas the Italian code demanded maximum publicity. Edward M. Wilson observed, however, that "this secret vengeance (or punishment) is really not so very secret" as "at least five people (the ragged man, Aurora, the Marquis, Batín and Lucrecia) know that Federico and Casandra have committed incestuous adultery together" (182). To this it might be retorted that Aurora and her fiancé, being part of the family, are also submitted to the duty of secrecy, and that the others do not count since they do not belong to the protagonists' peer group. It may be useful to examine this intriguing matter from a different, psychological and theological, angle.

One of the few respectable features in the character of Bandello's Marquis is that he allows the adulterers time enough to ponder, repent and redeem their sinful souls if they so wish: while Parisina keeps wallowing in evil, Ugo ensures his salvation. Lope went to great lengths in order to confer upon the static, unattractive character of this *macho* petty tyrant clearly outstanding qualities as a soldier of the Church, a loving father, and a responsible ruler. It comes as a surprise that he departed from the Bandello pattern for his ending. There must be some reason why the Spanish playwright caused this born-again nobleman — who, we must insist, is now eager to follow the path of righteousness, torn as he is between the rival claims of fatherly love and of his dual duty

El castigo sin venganza 67

to worldly honour and divine justice — to deprive the young sinners of any opportunity... for making their peace with God.[5] As the Duke himself reports in his last soliloquy, he goes to Casandra and tells her the reason for what he is about to do, whereupon she faints; he gags her, binds her hand and foot, and covers her with a cloth (2858-65). As soon as the Count enters, the Duke orders him to kill this nobleman who betrayed him and whose identity must remain secret (2927-53). Hardly has Federico complied when the father noisily summons his followers to kill his son for murdering his stepmother (2976-96). No more than some two hundred lines separate Casandra's last words (2775) from Federico's surprisingly astonished terminal question, "Why do they kill me?" (2997): a matter of minutes. At no point does the Duke display any concern with the eternal fate of his son and his wife. No doubt, it would not have been beyond Lope's dramatic ability to have him allow the culprits to repent, to confess under the seal of secrecy and thus to gain spiritual salvation, as Bandello had done. Why did the Spanish playwright alter his source material in this particular way?

According to José Antonio Maravall in *La cultura del Barroco*, the Spanish theatre, which "was almost wholly produced by priests, with the church's consent, and in its and the monarchy's service", shows that the Church occasionally "supported a nobiliary social morality that contradicted the evangelical message" (273, n. 54). In this respect *El castigo sin venganza* exemplifies a "baroque" syncretism that seeks to effect a reconciliation and a synthesis of (or a compromise between) Christian ideals and worldly conventions: the Duke's embarrassed casuistry on *castigo* and *venganza* should not disguise the plain fact that Lope turned the Bandello story into a *casus* in which the aristocratic honour code and Christian ethics conveniently lead to the same practical result: the execution of the sinners under the authority of the legitimate ruler to whom they happen to be related.

In 1632 the tragic outcome of the play was hailed by the censor himself as "a rare, exemplary case", because "it is written with truth and

---

[5] The only passage where clemency and pardon are mentioned (2842-45) is so obscure that, as Dixon and Parker have shown, it is equally possible to interpret it, with Karl Vossler (1932, 283), as meaning that the Duke hopes the harshness of the temporal punishment he is about to inflict will mitigate God's sentence in the other world, or, with Ramon Menéndez Pidal (145-48), that he hopes God will pardon him on account of the selfless moderation he shows in punishing them not in vengeful anger but in order to administer "la justicia santa/a un pecado sin vergüenza" (287-88).

due attention to the dignity of the Duke and the other characters" (Gigas, 603). Indeed, the bloody *desenlace* had enormous propaganda value because it was bound forcefully to impress on the collective mind of the popular audience the notion that infringement of the law, whether this- or other-worldly, is always fated to meet its due retribution. The honour code and the divine will are seen to co-operate as joint deterrents, which sinners disregard at their own peril. Lope went to inordinate lengths to show Federico and Casandra fully aware and fearful of the double risk, physical and supernatural, that they are running. This has the effect of enhancing the audience's sense of the overwhelming power of the temptation to which they finally surrender. While the modern reader is likely to identify the temptation with sex as Bandello did, it has another aspect as well, which no *siglo de oro* audience was likely to miss. The Duchess's primary motive is not sexual attraction, but revenge. That she should avenge her slighted pride by taking a lover did not seem as natural in the seventeenth century as it does now. As Melveena McKendrick points out:

> The social conventions which made honour the patrimony of the male made vengeance a masculine duty. Honour was his, and his the revenge when honour was lost. Strictly speaking, woman's role in this social structure was an instrumental one. She had no honour of her own that was distinguishable from virtue, but upon her virtue depended the honour of her male relations .... By taking the revenge upon herself, she not merely usurps the role played by the male in the maintenance of social order, but more important, reveals herself to be as sensible of honour as man himself, thereby presenting a direct challenge to the superiority of the male (261).

As a stage impersonation of *la mujer vengadora de su honor*, Casandra violates the norms of a society in which, in McKendrick's words, "husbands, unlike wives, were allowed their infidelities" (273). By taking vengeance in her own hands instead of calling on her natural male protector, her father, she displays an unacceptable conviction that marriage partners are equals and that either is dishonoured by the other's adultery. Casandra's lust for revenge subverts conjugal hierarchy; it must be seen as an even more potent force than adulterous sex in the intricate motivational structure that drives her to evil and ultimately leads her, together with her incestuous lover, to well-deserved elimination.

The modern reader's humanitarian sensitiveness may find the physical manner of their execution unduly tortuous and cruel. He should recall that Lope's contemporaries must have been even more aghast at its metaphysical consequences. Lope has arranged his material in such a way as to make it obvious that the adulterers embarked on their short career of criminal enjoyment in full consciousness that they were bound to be punished both by the Duke and by God. The *desenlace* most satisfactorily fulfils both expectations. The suddenness of their execution ensures damnation, thus rounding off the cosmic restoration of order which had been initiated by the Duke's conversion. In this sense, *El castigo sin venganza*, like Tirso de Molina's *El burlador de Sevilla*, offers an awesome reminder that no sinner should rely on the uncertain facility of eleventh-hour recantation.

The world of the play is a dual one, swayed by the demands of the Spanish honour code and Counter-Reformation morality. Whereas the Duke's subservience to the code is a characteristic shame-culture attitude, the lovers are not concerned with anything even remotely resembling Euripides' *eukleia*: when Casandra exclaims "tente, honor; fama, resiste" (2020), she knows she has already lost her soul and herself (2019, 2021). When Federico mentions the rumours in the palace (2273-75), his only preoccupation is to trick his father into disbelieving them. Conscience, the Senecan *pudor*, which instinctively revolts against the very thought of evil, seems to induce a genuine sense of guilt for a while when Federico, at the end of Act I, briefly recoils at the image of his bedding his own father's wife; this, however, is soon drowned in the whining preciosity of fear and self-pity. Whereas *pudor* and *ratio* are constantly associated in Seneca's Phaedra, what *razón* impresses on the minds of Lope's lovers is a clear knowledge of all they have to fear as a result of their prospective criminal behaviour.

This fear is temporarily overcome by lust for revenge and sex, only to recur with panicky intensity when they are really faced with the Duke's return. The text is calculated to expose Casandra's mad possessiveness and Federico's ignoble cowardice most mercilessly. At no point, however, does Lope attribute to his by now contemptible ex-heroes, feelings of remorse, or any sense of guilt, or any willingness to atone. Indeed, Federico's very last utterance as the Marquis kills him is his amazing question: "¡Oh padre! ¿Por qué me matan?" (2997).

In the debased minds of the incestuous adulterers, then, the only restraining force that thwarted their undesirable impulses for a while was the primitive fear of external castigation. The constant association of "el Duque" and "Dios" on their lips suggests that they do not see much difference between corporeal punishment and eternal damnation. Nor is this very surprising. In its policy of mass control, the medieval church had long manipulated the arts — painting, sculpture, morality plays, miracles, not to mention Dante's epic — in such a way as to imbue the imaginations of ordinary believers with a representation of otherworldly torments that is so graphically physical as to obliterate any sense of spiritual chastisement. God was to be feared; love of God was a monopoly of mystics and, perhaps, theologians. In its determination to restore the power of the Roman church, severely shattered by Renaissance humanism and the Reformation, the Council of Trent gave this trend new impetus and vitality. The theatre was used as a most efficient mass medium to this effect. Abundant evidence of this can be found in Jesuit drama throughout Europe. In the hands of outstanding playwrights the Spanish *comedia* became a major propaganda tool for spreading the theological and ethical doctrines of the church as well as the political and social ideology of absolute monarchy. As Rudolph Schevill pointed out half-a-century ago (119-20), it was the function of many *comedias* to propose stereotypes of conformity, to implant, through character depiction and plot development, assumptions that were consonant with the requirements of Church and State, and to counter the Renaissance spirit of free inquiry by restoring the authoritarian power of dogma. The artistic sophistication of the plays bolsters their exemplary value: the adulterers' fate is to be an *ejemplo* for Aurora (3000), the play itself an *ejemplo* (3021) for the Spanish people.

That this could be done with considerable subtlety and skill is obvious in *El castigo sin venganza*. There is no need to expatiate on Lope's artistry in describing the lovers' degradation from their early youthful innocence through the gradual response of their very human weakness to their final doom. The cautionary significance of the play resides in the careful depiction of the vulnerability of human will to the combined allurements of selfish desire and propitious circumstance, despite their better knowledge. On the whole, however, if we take advantage of the similarity in situation and plot, Federico and Casandra appear as definitely low-grade characters when compared with the classical Phaedras, both of whom acknowledge moral values higher than their own lives. Euripides' Phaidra hangs herself in the mistaken hope of preserving her reputation as a virtuous woman and the honour of her lineage. Seneca's Phaedra stabs herself in order to atone for a moral crime that never materialized and to expiate her share of responsibility in Hippolytus' death. But Federico's obsessional aim is just to stay alive. As to Casandra, she never even recognizes that her life is in danger and she dies absorbed in her distasteful mixture of vengeful pride and possessive lust. What is sadly missing is any trace of genuine inwardness, a rather uncomfortable observation after a thousand years of Christian indoctrination.

5

THE TRIUMPH OF GUILT:
RACINE'S *PHÈDRE* (1677)

We shall never know why Racine claimed that his *Phèdre* was "encore une tragédie dont le sujet est pris d'Euripide". It has long been realized that this unique masterpiece is largely a mosaic of quotations from Euripides and Seneca, transmuted, adapted and dove-tailed into a smooth coherence entirely its own. The texture of the plot, however, derives mainly from the Latin play, not merely on account of the centrality of the eponymous character, but chiefly because Racine allowed his Phèdre to outlive Hippolyte, thus giving himself the opportunity to elaborate her response to the consequences of her own deeds.

From the very beginning Racine follows Seneca in discarding Euripides' Olympian Prologue: the information conveyed by Aphrodite in the Greek play will be transferred to Phèdre's own speech at the end of I, iii. Like his Latin predecessor Racine found it inadvisable to give pagan gods and goddesses more than metaphorical status: they are not entitled to diegetic existence. As in Seneca it is Hippolyte who first appears on stage. But instead of the young man's long-winded outpourings about rural and athletic activities, Racine skilfully gives this first scene a genuine dramatic function. The dialogue between Hippolyte and Théramène is designed to provide basic information about the plot: Thésée's absence, Phèdre's mysterious illness and her seeming hostility to her stepson, the Prince's infatuation with Aricie despite his father's will. Two elements in this introductory scene deserve more attention than they have usually been awarded.

One is related to the character of Aricie, Racine's main original contribution to the cast. We can safely gloss over the lame justifications adduced by the playwright in his Preface. In fact an embarrassing problem for a seventeenth-century writer was to account for Hippolyte's chastity as given in the tradition. To present him as a frantic woman-hater as did Seneca contradicted the classical principle of decorum; to attribute his restraint to his devotion to Artemis as in Euripides gives the pagan goddess too effective a role; to have the Prince's heart engaged elsewhere was, despite all subsequent critical controversies, an elegantly simple way of giving his virtue a sound psychological foundation.

The second point has to do with Racine's manner of presenting Thésée's ambiguous character. The scene offers a balanced portrayal of the King as a model hero ("nobles exploits", 76) and a less than exemplary husband ("faits moins glorieux", 80). Racine asserted that he had found in Plutarch the motif of Thésée's philandering, of which there is no trace in the Greek play. Yet he was familiar with Seneca's account: the Latin Phaedra emphasized at an early stage (89-98) her husband's habitual profligacy as an extenuating circumstance for her own adulterous passion. The point is that in Racine's version this motif is dwelt upon by Hippolyte, not by Phèdre: not until the declaration scene will she so much as casually mention "ce volage adorateur de mille objets divers" (636). Such a transfer, slight though it may appear, is far from meaningless: it highlights the noble-mindedness of the French heroine, who does *not* seek extenuating circumstances. That Racine had little use for such a devious, tortuous character as Seneca's Phaedra is obvious from Phèdre's first appearance in I, ii, a scene which, with the remainder of Act I, is a fairly close replica of the Euripidean pattern.

Phèdre's arrival is prepared by Oenone, who describes the disorder in the Queen's mind and outward appearance as well as her own chagrin (143-51, 157-77; cf. *Hipp* 176-97). Phèdre herself voices her weariness (153-61) and nearly gives herself away as she inadvertently vents her yearning (176-78; *Hipp* 207-21) to the shocked surprise of the nurse, whose astounded "Quoi, Madame?" (179) neatly summarizes her Greek colleague's expatiations (*Hipp* 212-14, 222-26, 232-35). Phèdre then briefly pulls herself together (179-81; *Hipp* 239-41), only to return to her deep sorrow (182-84; *Hipp* 244-47). Oenone undertakes to extract the cause of the Queen's misery, blames her for her silence and lists reasons why it is her duty to stay alive (185-204; *Hipp* 284-310). Her mentioning the name of Hippolyte startles Phèdre (205-206; *Hipp* 310-12), whose aposiopesis is mistaken by the nurse for a sign of anger at her stepson (207-209; *Hipp* 312). The woman then exhorts the Queen to restore her health for the sake of her children (210-17; *Hipp* 313-14). To no avail. Phèdre returns to her lament, asserting that while she has no blood upon her hands, there is a stain in her heart (212-17; *Hipp* 323-14) and that she firmly intends to die rather than disclose its nature: the line "Je meurs pour ne point faire un aveu si funeste" (226) closely corresponds to the Greek Phaidra's explanation that death is a noble way out of her shameful predicament (*Hipp* 331). The reason for Racine's choice of Euripides rather than Seneca at this point is clear: his Phèdre is not to display the manipulative cunning of the Latin Phaedra; like her Greek model, she is to be totally innocent in the sense that her conscious mind is completely honest and sincere in its refusal to give way, or even utterance, to her unlawful passion.

Racine skipped the Euripidean Nurse's sophistry to the effect that if death is honourable, disclosure of its motivation can only enhance the Queen's good name (*Hipp* 332). Instead, Oenone proclaims her own death-wish (230-32) and effects the beseeching gesture (243-45; *Hipp* 333-35) that impels her mistress to make a full report:

> Quand tu sauras mon crime, et le sort qui m'accable,
> Je n'en mourrai pas moins, j'en mourrai plus coupable.
> (241-42)

The future tense signals a first step in Phèdre's evolution: however reluctantly, she is willing to talk, though she is still determined to die afterwards. On the face of it, the comparative form in the second line ("plus coupable") sounds like a typical shame-culture pronouncement. While it has no equivalent in Euripides, it might mean that disclosure, even to a trusted lower-class confidante, is a source of public knowledge, and therefore of shame. However, throughout the play Phèdre displays truly minimal concern with her reputation: such words as *honneur* and *gloire* hardly occur. Hers is a tragedy of inwardness and guilt. The phrasing merely reflects her awareness that giving verbal utterance to her feelings is tantamount to acknowledging, accepting, and even to intensifying them. By speaking out, she senses she will step over a threshold and reach a higher degree in culpability.

Phèdre's exordium to her confession closely follows the stichomythia in *Hippolutos*: the Queen first recalls the sorry fate of her mother Pasiphae (249-50; *Hipp* 337) and of her sister (Ariane 253-54; *Hipp* 339). In the family's female saga she sees herself as the third victim of Venus' anger (257-58); *Hipp* 343).[1] By the end of the dialogue, Oenone's earlier misunderstanding is cleared up and the name of the beloved revealed (262-64; *Hipp* 352-53). In the Greek play, the nurse at this point had voiced her horror and announced her own decision to die (*Hipp* 352-58); as Racine had already conveyed this death-wish in l. 230, Oenone now merely curses the "voyage infortuné" (267) which, as we shall presently learn, brought Phèdre from Athens to Troezen (302) and into the presence of her stepson. She thus provides a smooth transition to Phèdre's anamnesis: "Mon mal vient de plus loin" (269).

For Phèdre's account Racine found his material in Aphrodite's prologue in *Hippolutos*, but he introduced distortions which are worth considering in some detail.

After her marriage with Thésée Phèdre was taken to Athens where she first saw Hippolyte and fell in love with him (269-78; *Hipp* 24-28). In Euripides, she then had a temple built in Athens, which she dedicated to Cypris/Aphrodite; it was oriented in the direction of Troezen, whither — as the Greek audience could be expected to know — Theseus had sent the boy to be brought up by the local ruler, his grandfather Pitheus (*Hipp* 29-34). How this tallies with Phaidra's statement that her first plan was to conceal her love (*Hipp* 394) is not immediately obvious. Racine remedied this inconsistency by having his Phèdre build the temple not as an indirect hommage to Hippolyte but in order to propitiate Venus, to ward off the curse of her dreaded love and the attending "tourments inévitables"; in the hope, too, that her burnt offerings may incite the goddess to let her recover her "raison égarée" (279-82).

This apparently minor alteration provides an important clue to Racine's conception of Phèdre. In her rhesis the Greek Phaidra, we recall, listed three stages in her emotional-ethical development (*Hipp* 393-402): first, she did all she could to conceal her passion: second, she endeavoured to conquer it; when this proved impossible, she resolved to die. There is no such gradation in *Phèdre*: from the first, she recognizes the evil in her unlawful infatuation and she strives to

---

[1] Here Racine follows Seneca (*Phaed* 124-28): the mythical origin of Venus' hatred and curse is not her jealousy of Artemis as in Euripides, but the story, zestfully recounted by Homer, of her anger at the Sun-god's lack of discretion (see ch. 2, n. 1 above).

smother it. In this, we note, she complies with the moral advice dispensed by the Senecan *Nutrix*, who exhorted the Queen to "extinguish her flame" because it is easier to overcome love when resistance is immediate (*Phaed* 131-33). Clearly the Racinian heroine has no need for such advice.

After turning the building of the temple to this new purpose, Racine added an incident of his own devising. The text offers no reason whatsoever to doubt Phèdre's assertion that she went to extreme lengths in her determination to overcome her love: not only did she avoid Hippolyte's presence (289), she even feigned hatred for him (292-94) and went so far as to have him banished to Troezen (295-96). The purpose of such unobtrusive addenda to the tradition could only be to emphasize the relentless energy with which the Queen from the first strove to bring her dangerous impulses under control.

Racine's Preface warns us that his heroine is "neither entirely guilty nor entirely innocent". The phrase suggests that the purpose of the play is basically ethical and even judicial; yet, paradoxically, it prevents reader and audience from passing judgment on the main character. But Phèdre's first extended speech shows that on the contrary she is far from condoning the playwright's description: she considers herself both entirely innocent *and* entirely guilty. She is innocent because her first meeting with Hippolyte was brought about by chance ("Athènes me montra ...", 272). Nor has she been responsible for now joining him in Troezen: ironically, this is a result of Thésée's decision ("Par mon époux lui-même à Trézène amenée", 302). She did not yield to what she merely took to be an incipient infatuation; her failure has now revealed to her that it is not what she thought, the usual casual intervention of Venus in human affairs: she realizes that "Vénus tout entière" (306) has mustered all her dread power against her feeble self, now the sole target of the goddess's hatred against the Sun's progeny (249).

That she also feels entirely guilty becomes increasingly obvious as her reminiscences reach the present time. True, she knew from the beginning that Venus' flames are dangerous, a source of "tourments inévitables" (278). She soon realized that her emotions were contrary to reason (282), a malady (283), inflicting unfathomable misery (289). Yet it is not against chance or against Venus that she rebels, but against herself (291). And just after describing herself as an impotent victim of the goddess, she paradoxically concludes her speech in a mood of fierce self-indictment:

> J'ai conçu pour mon crime une juste terreur.
> J'ai pris ma vie en haine et ma flamme en horreur;
> Je voulais en mourant prendre soin de ma gloire,
> Et dérober au jour flamme si noire.
>
> (307-10)

Whereupon she beseeches Oenone to stop trying to divert her from her suicidal project. As will soon be made clear (I, v), the Nurse, contrary to her ancient models at this stage, is willing to comply; she even intends to follow her mistress to the tomb (337-39).

Unlike the Latin Phaedra's, Phèdre's death-wish is sincere: death, she trusts, will lift the unbearable tension between duty and passion in her schizoid self. In this, she is similar to Euripides' Phaidra. The latter, however, did not kill herself until the Nurse had informed Hippolutos of her feelings. What prevents the French heroine from immediately enacting her fatal decision is an incident invented by Racine: the report (erroneous, as it turns out) of Thésée's own death (I, iv). This is a major innovation which is intended to affect our assessment of the characters in a decisive manner. As Phèdre is now widowed, Oenone can argue without transgressing the bounds of law or accepted morality that her passion is no longer criminal. It is a measure of the French Phèdre's moral fastidiousness that she only half-heartedly agrees to desist from her death-wish, and for reasons which have nothing to do with the fulfilment of her sexual yearnings. Racine now abandons the Euripidean plot pattern to follow Seneca, though with alterations that must now be discussed.

Oenone's change of mind is in harmony with the externals of the Greco-Roman tradition. In Euripides the Nurse tries to deter Phaidra from her death-wish out of sheer love for her mistress and because she realizes that moral sermonizing is pointless. The Senecan *Nutrix* is shocked by Phaedra's feigned death-wish. In their different ways both then proceed to help the Queen gratify her incestuous longings. Oenone is the only one who changes her mind at this point *because the situation has changed*: her reasoning cannot incur moral blame, despite the element of legalistic sophistry that enters into it.

This, however, is only the second line of argument proffered by the nurse (349-53). She first enlarges at some length (343-48, 355-62) on a different reason, which is of a pragmatic order; it introduces the political theme that is Racine's most original contribution to the traditional tale. Oenone assumes that Hippolyte resents his stepmother's earlier show of hostility; at his father's death he will lawfully inherit Troezen, but in his lust for revenge and power, he may head a rebellion against Phèdre and try to conquer Athens, her own son's legal heirloom, which Aricie is probably eager to recover. Such speculations have been prepared for and prompted by Panope's brief speech in I, iv. They lead Oenone to point out that if Phèdre should also die, her orphaned son will have no one left to protect his rights or even his freedom. Oenone's conclusion is that Phèdre should abandon her death-wish and seek some arrangement with Hippolyte.

These innovations of Racine's have wide-ranging consequences both for the dramaturgy of the play and our appraisal of the characters. The plot now complies with the demand, central to French classical theory, that tragedy should deal with some *grande action d'Etat*: the private woes of Phèdre are linked with the political problem of Thésée's succession and of power-sharing in the Greek world. Though this also provides an additional function for Aricie alongside her love affair with Hippolyte and her role as a symmetric counterweight to Phèdre, it remains a subplot, suggesting that Racine, unlike Corneille, was more genuinely interested in personal psychology and ethics than in matters of political import. In this respect motherly concern for her son is now evinced as a morally laudable reason for Phèdre to meet Hippolyte personally and to enter into negotiations with him.

When Phèdre closes the act with her weary acquiescence in Oenone's advice, she conspicuously refrains from commenting upon the possible consequences of her widowhood upon the moral status of her passion and her future personal relationship with Hippolyte. There is no reason in the text to doubt her claim that "l'amour d'un fils" (365) is the only thing that can bring her back to life. By the end of Act I, then, Racine has established the fundamental innocence of Phèdre's conscious mind, which is the main reason why he chose to follow Euripides in the first place. The Queen's guiltlessness is enhanced by the fact that the motive for renouncing her death-wish derives from motherly love alarmed by political considerations. While she is thus exonerated from any conscious yielding to a passion that remains tainted in her eyes though it may no longer be technically unlawful, this momentous decision makes it possible, indeed perhaps mandatory, for Racine to join Seneca: Phèdre's *bona fide* renouncement of the death-wish leaves her exposed to temptation. From now on the plot as far as she is concerned parallels the career of her Latin namesake with its three crucial moments: her love declaration to her stepson, the slanderous accusation of Hippolyte after Thésée's return, and her confession and suicide following the Prince's death. Here again, however, the skilful mixture of borrowings and alterations provides a key to the specificity of Racine's purpose.

When Phèdre reappears on-stage to meet Hippolyte in II, 5, Racine avoided making use of the self-promptings ("Aude, anime", *Phaed* 592) which in the Latin play clearly indicate that her love declaration is a premeditated mandate. On the contrary, Phèdre's purpose in seeking this interview is truly to follow Oenone's advice and sollicit the Prince's protection for her son. In her introductory aside to Oenone she admits to her agitation: "J'oublie, en le voyant, ce que je viens lui dire" (582), thus incurring the nurse's pointed reminder (583). Commenting on this passage, André Gide misleadingly asserted that Phèdre, "se croyant veuve ... croit qu'elle va réussir à séduire Hippolyte. C'est à quoi elle va s'employer savamment, recourant à toutes ses ressources" (198). More recently Gordon Pocock concurred with Gide by asserting that "the alleged motive is a façade" invented by Racine "to make Phèdre more sympathetic" (258). Yet there is nothing in either text or context to support such a view. In Seneca Phaedra, posing as a weak widowed woman, opens the dialogue with a sham request for Hippolytus' protection (*Phaed* 609-23). It is the Prince who assures her of his lasting affection for his (half-)brothers (629-33). The Queen's hypocrisy is made obvious in a brief aside (634-35) showing her realization that she must be more explicit. She then confesses that she is consumed by a mad passion (638-44), which Hippolytus mistakenly assumes to be her "chaste love" for Theseus (645). This provides Phaedra with the needed opportunity to equivocate on her love for Theseus as a young man in such a way that her discourse becomes the open declaration that she intended to make from the first.

Racine follows this pattern, but the effect he creates is different because of seemingly minor alterations, especially in the first segment (586-608), which is considerably extended and falls into two parts. It is first made clear that Phèdre genuinely sought this interview solely in order to ensure her son's safety (586-90), as she will confirm after the declaration (696). Predictably, she then feels bound to explain why she fears Hippolyte's enmity in view of her feigned hostility in the past (591-604). She darkly concludes that:

> Si la haine peut seule attirer votre haine,
> Jamais femme ne fut plus digne de pitié.
>
> (606-607)

This disclaimer of enmity is the first hint of her true feelings that she gives Hippolyte. It is also the first evidence that her passion is beginning to take control of her discourse.

As in Seneca Hippolyte's innocent mind fails to take the cue, and he protests his benign understanding of Phèdre's suspicion (609-14), which incites the Queen to make an attempt at clarifying her meaning: Heaven, she says, has dispensed her from a rule that applies to most stepmothers (615-16). But she is driven to add incautiously that "un soin bien différent me trouble et me dévore" (617), an echo of *Phaed* 640-41. In Racine, too, the Prince assumes that his stepmother is alluding to her bereaved love for his father and he strives to console her by arguing that Thésée's death is by no means certain (618-22; *Phaed* 623-24, 644-45).

While at this point the French play has resumed its Senecan course, Phèdre dispenses with Phaedra's pointed remark that Pluto is not likely to allow the ravisher of his own spouse to escape (*Phaed* 627). But her observation that "l'avare Achéron ne lâche point sa proie" (626) is a terse translation of *Phaed* 634-35. Furthermore, whereas Hippolytus' denial had prompted Phaedra to an aside reiterating her sinful determination (*Phaed* 634-35), *Phèdre* lapses into a tell-tale expostulation: "il n'est point mort puisqu'il respire en vous" (627). As she realizes that she is on the verge of open disclosure, she pulls herself together — laying bare her deepest emotions at the same time: "je m'égare,/Seigneur: ma folle ardeur malgré moi se déclare" (629-30). This sequence of an unwilled confession precipitously followed by a denial that nevertheless confirms the avowal is redolent of lines 176-83, which also contain the key formula "malgré moi". There will be further examples of this microstructure which subtly convey the psychological processes at work in Phèdre's mind: the overpowering intensity of her passion, the torturing lucidity in her self-perception, her desperate moral uprightness.

In his persistant blindness, Hippolyte misses such implications and he marvels at Phèdre's wondrously burning love for his father (631-33) — an amazing misunderstanding which precipitates Phèdre into the lengthy declaration that occupies the second half of the Scene.

From the beginning of the interview, Seneca's Phaedra had proclaimed her determination to lead her stepson astray. On the contrary, Racine is intent on showing that the attempt at seduction is conducted by Phèdre despite herself. It is precisely the function of the recurrent microstructure to demonstrate by purely scenic means how her moral conscience and consciousness constantly react against the inroads of passion. This gives a new colouring to Phèdre's introductory lines, which are largely borrowed from the Latin play: "Oui, Prince, je languis, je brûle pour Thésée./Je l'aime.../Charmant, jeune..." (634-39) unmistakably echo Seneca's "Hippolyte, sic est: Thesei vultus amo/illos priores suos tulit quondam puer" (*Phaed* 646-47). For Phaedra, this description of her alleged — or rather quondam — love for Theseus is a rhetorical device preparatory to the Theseus-Hippolytus identification. In Phèdre, it is a desperate attempt to disguise her lapse by confirming Hippolyte in his notion that "soin bien différent" (617) refers to her lost husband. But the conclusion is the same in both plays and the father-son identification is couched in similar language:

> tuaeque Phoebes vultus aut Phoebi mei,
> tuusque potius – talis, en talis fuit
>
> (*Phaed* 654-55)

is tersely echoed in Phèdre's "Tel qu'on dépeint nos dieux, ou tel que je vous voi" (640). But the sudden explicitness in "tuusque potius" is a step forward in Phaedra's execution of her self-assigned mandate, whereas Phèdre's "ou tel que je vous voi" should be uttered (after a marked caesura) as a kind of aside: the Queen's inner thought, which she voices almost involuntarily, in a trancelike state of half-consciousness.

The second section of Phèdre's declaration elaborates the Thésée-Hippolyte identification. This, too, follows the Senecan pattern. The Queen first expatiates on the physical and moral similarities between her stepson and the young Theseus (640-51; *Phaed* 656-60). She then conjures up an image of Hippolyte, rather than his father, visiting Crete to destroy the Minotaur. In either case this leads to further superimposition: the remembrance of what actually happened when the Queen's sister helped Theseus fades into a phantasmatic image of Ariane guiding Hippolyte (645-52; *Phaed* 661-62). But while in Seneca this is followed by Phaedra's overt, impassioned declaration (656-71),

Racine inserts a further hypothetical shift, in which the Ariane-Hippolyte image is supplanted by an image of Phèdre herself guiding Hippolyte inside the labyrinth:

> Mais non, dans ce dessein je l'aurais devancée...
> Et Phèdre au labyrinthe avec vous descendue
> Se serait avec vous retrouvée ou perdue.
>
> (653-62)

The phrase "ou perdue" is distinctly anticlimactic. As Martin Turnell observed in *The Classical Moment* (206), and confirmed in *Jean Racine: Dramatist* (264), it "marks the passing of the trance and the return to the actual world". We may doubt, however, that this "return to reality" is accompanied by what Turnell described in the former work (though not in the latter) as "a shattering sense of disillusionment" which is "underlined" by Hippolyte's shocked response — in André Gide's words, "la froideur avec laquelle Hippolyte-Joseph accueille cette proposition" (199). I rather think that the dying fall marks the return of Phèdre's moral consciousness, the realization that union with her stepson ("retrouvée") is her moral loss. And it is this return, not "to the actual world", but to the world of ethical truth, which makes her receptive to Hippolyte's indignant reaction (663-64; *Phaed* 671-97).

The Prince's brief exclamation (663-64) summarizes his tirade in Seneca (682-98). For Racine, it is an opportunity to have Phèdre pull herself together once more. In a weak, obviously futile endeavour to convince her stepson that he again misunderstands her, she haughtily invokes the concern with reputation with which, as a Queen and a virtuous woman, she is supposed to be endowed: "Aurais je perdu tout le soin de ma gloire?" (666) — her second and last reference to *gloire*. But Racine's Phèdre is not a shame-culture person as was Euripides' Phaidra. The social criterion, the fear of outward disapproval, has always mattered less to her than the inner valuation of her demanding moral sense. While Hippolyte — with some confusion and perhaps out of sheer politeness, or even merely in the hope that this is a god-sent opportunity for bringing the embarrassing conversation to an end — apologizes and prepares to depart (667-70), she realizes that the unintended, yet increasingly unmistakable message has, in Turnell's apt phrase, "gone home". There is no longer any point in trying to conceal the ugly truth, and she explodes into the ultimate avowal:

> Ah! cruel, tu m'as trop entendue!
> Je t'en ai dit assez pour te tirer d'erreur.
> Eh bien! connais donc Phèdre et toute sa fureur.
> J'aime.
>
> (670-73)

Phèdre has two conceivable reasons for taxing the Prince with cruelty. One is that his rebuke frustrates her yearning; the other, that she cannot but resent the note of moral contempt in his rejection. Like the Latin Phaedra's, her speech after his reaction focuses on the tragic paradox of her predicament, torn as she is between her passion and her moral sense. Here again Racine follows Seneca while departing from his model in unobtrusive, yet significant, ways.

In her first two lines (*Phaed* 698-99), Seneca's heroine restates her understanding of her situation: plagued like her mother by a curse which has compelled her to love what she should shun, she has no control over herself. She then devotes four lines (700-704) to her steadfast determination to follow her stepson everywhere. In the French tragedy order and proportion are reversed. A single word, "J'aime", is enough to convey the depth and intensity of Phèdre's passion. After this, however, she indulges in an outburst of self-loathing (673-98) designed to convince Hippolyte ("Ne pense pas ...") that she does not deserve his contempt since her conscious self never acquiesced either in her love or in the tell-tale words it has pressed on her lips, including the final avowal, "J'aime":

> Cet aveu que viens de faire,
> Cet aveu si honteux, le crois-tu volontaire?
>
> (693-94)

The pathetic question follows what is practically a rehearsal of her reminiscences to Oenone in I, iii: after forcefully proclaiming her moral revulsion against her pulsions (674-78), she recalls the responsibility of the gods (679-82), her desperate attempts to resist her passion (683-86) and their fruitlessness (687-92). The question also announces her updating of the narrative: she had sought this interview in order to obtain Hippolyte's protection for her son, but "Hélas! je ne t'ai pu parler que de toi-même" (695-96).

The function of Phèdre's speech so far has been to emphasize the dialectical combination of lust and repression at a moment when she can still be regarded as technically innocent, since she condemns herself and since Hippolyte's outspoken rejection stands in the way of any fulfilment of her objectionable yearnings. Equally meaningful is the way Racine, obviously writing with the Senecan text in front of him, chose to depart from it in the sword episode which concludes the dialogue in both tragedies.

In the Latin play, after Hippolytus has conveyed his loathing with his usual magniloquent rhetoric (*Phaed* 671-97) and after his stepmother has renewed her profession of love (700-703), the young man, fearing for his own chastity, bursts out in righteous wrath and draws his sword to inflict upon his father's wife the punishment she deserves (704-709). Phaedra then proclaims her relief at dying by his hand with her conscience safe (710-12), whereupon the Prince changes his mind and announces in disgust that he will not grant her such favour: he relinquishes his "polluted sword" and flees to his beloved "woods and wild beasts" (713-18), thus providing an opportunity for the Nurse to concoct and publicize her slanderous plot while Phaedra is lying in a swoon (718-35).

In the French play Hippolyte remains silent and Phèdre herself draws the logical conclusion of her self-indictment. Racine places on her lips words of reproof that Seneca had attributed to Hippolytus. It is she who commands the Prince to "take revenge" and "punish her" (699; *Phaed* 671-74). It is she who voices his alleged sense of being offended and defiled. It is she who describes herself as a "frightful monster" (701, 703; *Phaed* 688), whose killing will make him worthy of his father's heroic exploits (700; *Phaed* 696). And it is she who realizes that her "vile blood" is unworthy of being shed by his hand (707-10; *Phaed* 713-18). Racine thus drives Phèdre step by step to take Hippolyte's sword in her own hands in a final attempt to rid the world of her impure, loathsome self. Hers has never been a feigned death-wish. Her last gesture in this scene confirms how sincere she was when she announced her impending death at the beginning of the dialogue: the sword episode belies Maurice Delcroix's ingenious but half-hearted hypothesis that "l'évocation de sa mort prochaine peut n'être qu'une forme inconscience de coquetterie, ou la ruse d'une marâtre qui n'a que cette chance d'être pardonnée" (158 n.). The example of Seneca's *Phaedra* demonstrates that a playwright, even of average dramatic skill, has a number of ways to convey such tortuous goings-on at the back of a character's mind.

Act III is when Phèdre's integrity really begins to falter. The central problem of the play is the apportionment of culpability and responsibility in criminal behaviour. Throughout the first two Acts Phèdre is shown to have been carried away despite her better knowledge and against her conscious will. Her tragic awareness that she is unable to live in harmony with her upright principles leads her to an impasse the only issue from which is death. Only the timely intervention of Oenone has prevented her from stabbing herself. It is not difficult to grasp why Racine departed from the Senecan pattern and postponed the Nurse's mendacious proposal until the next Act. The demands of psychological verisimilitude made it imperative to show how Phèdre's hitherto unswerving moral judgment becomes prepared to allow, however passively, Oenone to have it her own way. Like the Senecan heroine Phèdre follows an inexorably descending slope towards evil. But whereas the former's conscious mind had consistently connived with her impassioned self, Phèdre's moral sense has consistently resisted her objectionable desires. Since Racine's conception of the Queen's character was different from that of Seneca, he needed to contrive some dramatic device to account for the psychological evolution required by the externals of the plot.

Phèdre's inner change appears at the outset of III, i when she starts blaming Oenone: "Importune, .../De quoi viens-tu flatter mon esprit désolé?" (737-38). Her disapproval relates to two things. She is obviously angry because the Nurse saved her life; as she ruminates over her stepson's revulsion, she is filled with shame (746) and bewails the fact that she is still alive: "Pourquoi détournais-tu mon funeste dessein?" (757); reaching further back into the past of I, v, she insists on the Nurse's responsibility in what she regards as her recent lapses: "Toi-même, rappelant ma force défaillante, .../ Par tes conseils flatteurs tu m'as su ranimer" (769-71). In retrospect Oenone appears to her distracted mind as one of the external agents that have wiled her away from the straight path of duty. But the blame in line 738 also refers to a piece of advice offered off-stage and presently to be repeated as Oenone chides Phèdre for a display of self-pity which can only fan a fire that she ought to quench (753-54). With her pragmatic mind she again urges the Queen to ban Hippolyte from her thoughts and to concentrate on the worthier task of assuming the guidance of the state (755-58).

Because of the long critical tradition of deprecating Oenone — a tradition initiated by Phèdre herself in this passage and seemingly condoned in Racine's Preface — it is important to insist that, contrary to the Senecan *Nutrix*, her devotion has so far constantly prompted her to eminently commonsensical and morally unimpeachable counselling. It is Phèdre who rejects her advice when she retorts that she cannot hope to rule over the state since she cannot rule over herself (759-62). She reverts to her obsessive passion with a sense that her crime is now beyond repair: "De l'austère pudeur les bornes sont passées" (766), a fine rendering of Seneca's "Serus est nobis pudor" (*Phaed* 595), but this was said by Phaedra *before* the declaration. Furthermore, a new element intervenes as Phèdre unexpectedly declares that the mere fact of giving utterance to her shameful love has generated hope in her heart:

> J'ai déclaré ma honte aux yeux de mon vainqueur,
> Et l'espoir malgré moi s'est glissé dans mon coeur.
> (767-68)

The use of the Present Perfect rather than the Simple Past intimates that this hope, hitherto unmentioned, is still present in the Queen's heart. It is probably this which prompts Oenone, after a brief, almost casual attempt at self-defence (773-74), to undertake destroying her mistress's unconscionable passion by offering an exceedingly negative image of Hippolyte: she insists on his alleged cruelty, stern obstinacy and heinous pride, and she hints that his disdain is a mortal offence to Phèdre's dignity (775-79). This is palpably untrue, yet it may also be the way the good woman, shocked by her mistress's distressing failure, really perceived the situation: "Que Phèdre en ce moment n'avait-elle mes yeux?" (780).

Her arguing is all the more ineffectual as Phèdre is now overwhelmed by her newer hope. Hippolyte, she says, may discard his pride; his silence may be due to surprise as he was hearing words of love for the first time in his life (781-86). To all of which Oenone can only reply by borrowing the Senecan *Nutrix*'s words of admonition, "Genus omne profugit" (*Phaed* 243): "Il a pour tout le sexe une haine fatale" (789). Phèdre's immediate reply also comes from Seneca's "Paelicis careo metu" (*Phaed* 243): "Je ne me verrai point préférer de rivale" (790). The scene is a major step towards Phèdre's moral downfall: her wilful surrender to passion. The future tense in line 790 shows that she is now planning for a new phase, in which Oenone's cautious advice and her well-meant moralizing have become definitely obsolete: "Enfin, tous ces conseils ne sont plus de saison" (791). It is she who deliberately orders the Nurse to change her course: "Sers ma fureur, Oenone, et non point ma raison" (792). And she lays down the broad lines of a strategy which is not so much designed to arouse love in Hippolyte as vilely to play on his alleged power-seeking (793-806): she instructs the newly-appointed go-between to resort to any means whatsoever (807) to win him round. She even advises her to stir his compassion by shameless posturing: the Nurse is urged to insist, weep, wail, beseech, and even to pretend that her mistress is on the threshold of death (809-10) — even though Phèdre is now obviously at her most energetic, assuring the Nurse with regal self-confidence and authority that she will endorse whatever the latter may do (811).

R.C. Knight legitimately admired Racine's art in fusing "l'héroïne éhontée de Sénèque et l'héroïne pudique d'Euripide" (1952, 343). Coming right in the middle of the play, III, i is the exact moment when the Euripidean heroine of the first two Acts turns Senecan. Hope and action are now substituted for the earlier death-wish; Phèdre's conscious mind is now subordinated to her passion and argues along lines set by her Latin model *at the beginning* of the play: her offer of a political bribe, sovereignty over Athens, and her appeal to compassion come from Seneca (*Phaed* 617-23). The political theme allows Racine to make his Phèdre even more ignoble than Seneca's: she goes so far as to use her own son as an instrument, giving Hippolyte authority over him. The pointed reference to the Senecan *furor-ratio* antinomy confirms that her lawless urge has contaminated a further layer of her personality: in her invocation to Venus (III, ii) she shows herself to be still aware, at an ethical-intellectual level, that hers is a criminal passion; her mind is still able to fathom "the depths of shame" (813) to which she has now stooped, but her conscious will has completely surrendered to Venus ("ton triomphe est parfait" (816). In I, iii she had implored the goddess to spare her and allow her to recover her reason (279-82); with ingenuous cunning she now invites her to gain new glory and avenge herself by subduing Hippolyte, a "more rebellious enemy" of love, ending her soliloquy with the climactic assertion that "our cause is one" (817-22). Here again, significantly, Racine has Phèdre use arguments that Seneca had placed on the lips of the Nurse (*Phaed* 413-22).

Phèdre's new-born hope is brutally crushed when Oenone comes back with the news of Thésée's return (III, iii). The Nurse's immediate spontaneous advice is for the Queen to stifle her now pointless love and to revert to her past virtue (825-26). This is not as easy as her shallow mind seems to assume. As she sets out in excitement to describe the King's arrival, Phèdre, to her astonishment (835, 839), bluntly cuts her and reiterates her death-wish.

In its original formulation in I, iii, the motivation for the death-wish was twofold: Phèdre had decided to die in order to preserve her *gloire* (309) and to cleanse the universe of her impure flame (310). What matters to her now is her *honneur*, her good name. Her passion was in itself an insult to Thésée's honour, her avowal has destroyed her own reputation:

> J'ai fait l'indigne aveu d'un amour qui l'outrage;
> . . . .
> Je mourais ce matin digne d'être pleurée;
> J'ai suivi tes conseils, je meurs déshonorée.
>
> (833-38)

While the Queen once more blames the nurse, her unusual concern with the outward criterion of public approval may have been intended by Racine as further indication of moral degradation. Anyhow, it is not surprising that the French playwright now turns back to the Euripidean model and to the Greek heroine's shame-culture motivations. The double mirror image in ll. 841-42 —

> Je verrai le témoin de ma flamme adultère
> Observer de quel front j'ose aborder son père

— makes apposite use of Hippolutos' threat to the Nurse (*Hipp* 660-62); Phèdre's fear that her stepson will report to his father (845-48) had already been voiced by Phaidra (*Hipp* 689-90); her protestation that she knows herself, that she is incapable of sinning with a tranquil mind, her sense that even the walls of the palace are awaiting Thésée to undeceive him (849-56) all come from the Greek Phaidra's rhesis (*Hipp* 405, 413-14, 415-18) when she explained why she had rather die than incur public reproof. But Phèdre's discourse has greater urgency since she has already confessed her love to the Prince; and her fear lest her children should inherit a sullied name (860-68) reverberates a preoccupation that Phaidra uttered both at the end of the rhesis (*Hipp* 419-23) and as she was about to hang herself (*Hipp* 715-18).

In her aversion to publicity the Greek Phaidra was unaware that Hippolutos had sworn never to reveal the Nurse's vicarious declaration (*Hipp* 605, 611). Both the French Phèdre and Oenone underestimate the noble-mindedness of the Prince, who has vowed that the dreadful secret shall remain buried in oblivion (719-20). Indeed, Oenone, with her quick-witted practicality — or rather Racine, all-time world champion of smooth transitions — avails herself of her mistress's fear on behalf of her children to point to the gap in her reasoning and to turn fright into panic: "Il n'en faut point douter ..." (869). The Queen's death, she observes, will inevitably give more credibility to Hippolyte's malevolent accusation, and she, a mere servant, will have no authority to contradict him (869-78). And she links up with an alarming picture of the Prince's triumph as he gleefully spreads the news of dead Phèdre's shameful passion (879-80). Oenone's line, "Et conter votre honte à qui voudra l'ouïr" (680) is an adaptation of the Greek Phaidra's self-warning, "He will fill all the land with tales of my shame" (*Hipp* 691). The Nurse's speech is ambiguous in its motivation. On one hand, it is in line with her ingrained devotion to the Queen's life and good name and to the safety and political rights of her children. On the other hand, there seems to be an element of manipulation in her depiction of Hippolyte's future triumph. Indeed it presently appears that the intention at the back of her mind has been to condition her mistress so as to prepare her to receive her own, glaringly criminal, proposal. The speech leads to the cautious question, "do you love him still?/How do you view" him? (882-83), eliciting Phèdre's fateful reply that Hippolyte is now "a frightful monster" in her eyes (814).

The new, terrifying image of the Prince in Phèdre's mind enables Racine to give psychological plausibility to her acquiescing in the vile scheme that is to be propounded, as in Seneca, by the Nurse. Significantly however, the Preface does not call on Seneca's authority to justify this departure from Euripides:

> I have been at pains to make [Phèdre] slightly less odious than in the tragedies of the ancients, where she resolves of her own accord to accuse Hippolytus. I felt that calumny was somewhat too low and foul to be put in the mouth of a princess whose sentiments were otherwise so noble and virtuous .... Phèdre consents to it only because she is in such a state of excitement as to be out of her mind (trans. Cairncross, 245).

In this account of the writer's motives psychological plausibility ranks uppermost and is closely linked with the classical notion of socio-ethical decorum. In fact, Racine followed the Latin model: why, Oenone argues, should the Queen concede victory to her stepson (885; *Phaed* 719) when she can throw the blame upon him in the first place (886-87; *Phaed* 720-21)? The evidence is there (888; *Phaed* 730): the young man's sword (889; *Phaed* 729) and the Queen's own agitation (890; *Phaed* 731-32) — to which for good measure Racine adds Phèdre's past grief and her ostentatious hostility to Hippolyte, whose exile she had engineered (890-92). But while the Senecan Nurse speaks in the first person plural ("regeramus", "arguamus", *Phaed* 720-21), Oenone uses the imperative mood: "Osez l'accuser ..." (886). This seems to be an exceedingly slight modulation, yet it enables Racine to provide a striking illustration of Phèdre's constant wobbling between emotional urge and moral principle. She has just described her stepson as "a frightful monster", but when she is invited to defend herself against his potential accusations, she is once again impelled to an abrupt turn-around and she bursts out indignantly: "Moi, que j'ose opprimer et noircir l'innocence!" (893). This vehement intrusion of Phèdre's conscience compels Oenone subtly to alter her scheme: she is the one who will utter the calumny — "Mon zèle n'a besoin que de votre silence/... Je parlerai" (894, 899) — thus joining the Senecan model.

Oenone is at the centre of this scene, which illuminates her unduly maligned character. Racine himself pointed out that her motivation is her total devotion to her mistress. But there is more to it than that, and analysts should not overlook the fact that her humble mind is also the seat of a genuine inner conflict between her devotion to the Queen and her own moral sense. The text offers no reason to doubt her sincerity when she asserts that she feels remorse at her proposal and that she had rather die a thousand deaths rather than blacken the innocent Prince's good name (896-97): the ugly lie is unfortunately necessary to protect the Queen's life (898-99). In an attempt to alleviate her (and Phèdre's) remorse she almost casually fancies that Thésée's anger will demand no more than some mild castigation (899-902); but, she goes on, should Hippolyte's blood be shed (903), Phèdre's threatened honour requires that much: "pour sauver votre honneur combattu,/Il faut immoler tout, et même la vertu" (903-908).

Oenone's speech neatly outlines the order of her priorities: her life is less important than her own integrity, which in turn is less important than her mistress's life even at the cost of Hippolyte's good name, which she proposes to sully; the Prince's very life matters less than Phèdre's honour. Total loyalty to the Queen is Oenone's highest value to which everything must be sacrificed, including "la vertu" in an absolute sense: what is at stake here is not solely the Nurse's own personal integrity: it is also Phèdre's, and her stepson's reputation as well.

As father and son now appear (Oenone: "je vois Thésée"; Phèdre: "Ah! je vois Hippolyte", 909), the Queen's confusion is at its apex. She is aware of this: "Dans le trouble où je suis, je ne puis rien pour moi" (912); and she passively allows the nurse to have it her own way: "Fais ce que tu voudras ..." (911). However, she cannot avoid greeting her husband. It is her bewildered mood — not what Jean Pommier called her "jésuitisme" (219) — which is reflected in her confused and confusing words (913-20). She informs Thésée that she has been a victim of "jealous fortune", that she no longer deserves his love and that her honour has been slighted. This ambiguous confession leaves much in the dark, especially the nature of the offence and the identity of the offender. As a result Thésée will be plunged in an abyss of perplexity (979-82), Hippolyte will fear that she intends to incriminate herself (98-90), and Oenone will later be able to claim, by way of introduction to the calumny, that Phèdre was merely attempting to spare her husband (1014). Everything in the text conspires to prevent the reader from deciding whether the equivocation is a genuine reflection of Phèdre's mental confusion or an astute device of her conscious mind. If the former, the brief speech should be taken as a tentative anticipation of her final confession; if the latter, as a preparation for her further degradation in the immediate future.

When the curtain rises on Act IV, Oenone has already informed Thésée, off-stage, of the alleged nature of his dishonour; her reply to the King's anguished questioning confirms that she sticks to the plan elaborated at the end of III, iii. When Thésée interprets his wife's "silence" (referring to her ambiguous greeting) as an attempt to spare his son, the Nurse cleverly retorts that "Phèdre épargnait plutôt un père déplorable" (1014), and concludes with the self-serving (though in fact truthful) assertion: "Moi seule à votre amour j'ai su la conserver" (1020). As far as Phèdre's character is concerned, however, Act IV is all the more important as it has no model in the classical tradition: it may therefore be assumed that this peripeteia, which further delays the dénouement, has some specific function pertaining to Racine's own purpose.

When Phèdre comes to Thésée (IV, iv) after overhearing his deadly call on Neptune (IV, iii), her overt purpose is to save Hippolyte's life. She first appeals to the King's moral sense: shedding his son's blood by his own hand is a most horrible crime (1170-71),[2] which Thésée indeed assures her he does not contemplate (1175). She also appeals to his compassion for her: she would feel responsible for such a crime (1173-74). There is no evidence so far for Bernard Weinberg's assertion (261) that "Phèdre comes to Thésée in order to make ... a confession, and ... is about to conform to her principle that she could not 'opprimer et noircir l'innocence' (893)". As she presently admits to herself, she was prompted by "remorse" (1218), but in retrospect she fears that she might have been driven to accuse herself and unveil the dreadful truth (1198-1202). This is all hypothetical. One thing is clear: contrary to Seneca's, Racine's heroine is not yet ready to make a clean breast. What definitely precludes such a contingency is Thésée's abrupt revelation that Hippolyte is in love with Aricie.

There may have been many reasons why Racine grafted the character of Aricie onto the traditional cast: loading the slender plot with some extra ore, providing an image of innocent love as a foil to Phèdre, introducing a motive acceptable to the modern mind for Hippolyte's rejection. In connection with Phèdre's character and evolution, Scenes iv and v of Act IV show that Aricie introduces a new psychological element, jealousy, which initiates a further step in the Queen's moral decline. In her soliloquy (IV, iv), she describes the unexpected news as a "thunderstroke" which rekindles the ashes of a "feu mal étouffé" (1193-95). In a turn-around not unprecedented in Racine,[3] Phèdre's possessiveness, fanned by jealousy, turns sour. It is now loaded with resentment as she renounces any intention to defend the Prince (1213). A new element comes to the fore in her wavering mood: wounded pride. Contrary to what she thought, Hippolyte is not immune to love, but his love goes to Aricie, not to her (1203-204). In her blind anger she turns to hasty generalizing: her stepson's heart is easy to move, but she is

---

[2] When assessing degrees of guilt, it is important to remember that the old taboo against shedding one's own blood was still operational in seventeenth-century dramatic convention: it accounts for the Duke of Ferrara's bizarre device for having his son killed without staining his own hands. Racine's Thésée refrains from killing Hippolyte himself lest "ta mort encor, honteuse à ma mémoire,/De mes nobles travaux vienne souiller la gloire" (1056-57): to have Neptune do the job ("Etouffe dans son sang ses désirs effrontés", 1075) is no violation of the taboo.

[3] See for example Hermione's changing attitude to Pyrrhus in *Andromaque*.

the only woman he cannot bear (1211-12). The exalted image of the Prince she had pictured in her love declaration makes room for equally exalted deprecation. She even resorts to Oenone's own words (when the woman was trying to dampen her dangerous passion) as she depicts his ungratefulness (1205, cf. 757), his "cruel eyes" (1210, cf. 777) and his overweening pride (1206, cf. 779). After Thésée's return, the nurse had impressed upon her a view of Hippolyte as "a frightful monster" (884). Scene v is a soliloquy and its purpose is to show that Phèdre, under the impact of jealousy and wounded pride, has now integrated this hateful image, just as her former soliloquy (III, vi) was designed to convey her willing acceptance of her dubious passion prior to Thésée's return.

In the ensuing dialogue with Oenone (IV, vi) the Queen first rehearses her past sorrows, but she insists that she is now being submitted to the worst torment she has ever experienced (1225-30). She almost casually blames Oenone for failing to inform her of Hippolyte's infatuation with Aricie (1233-34), a most unfair accusation since the Nurse's exclamations at lines 1219 and 1225 are sufficient evidence of her ignorance and good faith. As Phèdre fantasies about the lovers' bliss (1236-40), she emphasizes the contrast with the agony of frustration and guilt in her own soul.

With her down-to-earth, lower-class commonsense, Oenone, trying as hard as ever to console her mistress, flatly observes that the young pair's vain love will do them no good since they will never meet again (1251-52). The woman's plain good will cannot be questioned, but her rather tasteless allusion to Hippolyte's imminent exile and perhaps death prompts Phèdre to exclaim romantically, "Ils s'aimeront toujours" (1262). The very thought drives her to an acme of frenzied fury. In a new fit of trance-like exaltation she voices what is truly her basest impulse, a murderous lust for revenge:

> Non, je ne puis souffrir un bonheur qui m'outrage,
> Oenone; prends pitié de ma jalouse rage;
> Il faut perdre Aricie, il faut de mon époux
> Contre un sang odieux réveiller le courroux.
> Qu'il ne se borne pas à des peines légères:
> Le crime de la soeur passe celui des frères.
> Dans mes jaloux transports je le veux implorer.
> (1257-63)

The helpless Queen once more appeals to her dear Nurse for compassion and help, but the initiative this time is uncontrovertibly hers: hers the evil determination to destroy Aricie; hers, too, the nauseating idea of using her own husband's enmity to the girl's family as the instrument of her vengeful jealousy. Phèdre's fate follows a sinusoidal course of steadily increasing amplitude as she evolves from pardonable lapses for which she is not responsible (her meeting Thésée's son, her passion itself, the avowal to Oenone, the love confession to Hippolyte) to increasingly unacceptable obedience to ever baser impulses: when she connives with Venus despite her sense of shame and when she acquiesces in Oenone's slanderous scheme, which the Nurse herself declares to be contrary to virtue. The planning of Aricie's destruction represents the nadir in her carefully phased moral degradation.

As has by now become usual, Phèdre's conscience recoils immediately and regains control. The familiar microstructure is repeated ("Que fais-je?", 1264) as she suddenly becomes aware of the implications of her plan. These she lists with relentless acumen and concludes:

> Mes crimes désormais ont comblé la mesure.
> Je respire à la fois l'inceste et l'imposture.
>
> (1264-70)

And she recoils in unprecedented dread from the judgment of the all-seeing gods, her ancestors: the "sacré soleil" from which she springs, Jupiter who is her grandsire, all her forebears who fill the sky and the universe, are witness to her transgressions (1273-76). Even death cannot hide her from their sight, since her own father, Minos, administers justice in hell (1280), and he is bound to seek new tortures to punish the abominable crimes of his daughter (1286-89). As the image of her father impresses itself on her horrified imagination with growing immediacy, she weakly tries to stir his compassion and asks him to pardon her: after all, she contends, she was the victim of divine wrath and she never enjoyed the fruits of her shameful passion (1289-32). Yet this reiterated recognition of innocence, both in motivation and in deed, does not mollify her conscience any more than it is likely to placate her father's judgment. She again repeats her proleptic assertion of impending death as the only way out of her predicament: "Je rends dans les tourments une pénible vie" (1294).

In a new, and as it turns out ultimate, attempt to save her mistress's life, Oenone dismisses Phèdre's latest and most heinous crime, the plot against Aricie, as "une excusable erreur" (1296) — presumably because it was just an ephemeral phantasm of her sick imagination and no actual misdeed has been committed. As the Nurse bluntly puts it, the only palpable fact is that Phèdre is in love: "Vous aimez" (1297). Starting from this premise, the good woman invites the Queen to take a different view of the whole matter (1296) and proceeds to develop an argument aimed at reviving her erstwhile hopes and remedying the sense of sexual frustration she has just openly expressed.

This signals a change in Oenone herself. So far she has repeatedly tried to divert Phèdre from a passion that became hopeless after Hippolyte's rejection (753-54) and unmistakably criminal after Thésée's return (825-26). The new stance she is about to formulate recreates a situation that parallels the early scene in *Hippolutos* when the Nurse set out to erase Phaidra's "high-flown" discourse (*Hipp* 490) and advised her to "dare accept this love" (*Hipp* 476). The comparison brings out another aspect of Racine's peculiar talent for softening his characters' utterances that Leo Spitzer once called *Dämpfung*. Oenone cannot be as crudely outspoken as her Greek model was in asserting that "men should not aim at perfection in life" (*Hipp* 467), but in the same advocacy of *mêden agan* wisdom, the same spirit of compromise, she uses the same arguments for the same purpose: the Queen is subjected to a fate assigned by some supernatural power (1297-98; *Hipp* 438); hers is not an unheard-of case (1299; *Hipp* 437-38); she is not the only victim of the irresistible power of sex (1300; *Hipp* 440-50); being human she must accept the weaknesses inherent in man's condition (1301-2; *Hipp* 467-72); and in conclusion, she reminds her mistress that even the gods on Olympus "Ont brûlé quelquefois de feux illégitimes" (1304-5; *Hipp* 451-56), a climactic argument which Seneca had inserted in his own Phaedra's sophistical attempt at self-defence (*Phaed* 186-94).

The differences between Racine's handling of the scene and Euripides' are equally revealing. First, we note that the French playwright discarded the Greek Nurse's lewd innuendoes about love philtres that could put an end to Phaidra's troubles (*Hipp* 509-10). More important, however, is the fact that Racine transferred this scene to a late phase in the action. In both classical plays, the Nurse rallies to the Queen's illicit passion at an early stage because the latter's death-wish frightens her out of her early moralizing stance. It is for the same reason that Oenone now proffers her most unpalatable suggestion: the Queen should stop blaming herself, she should acknowledge her human weakness, and she should accept her impassioned attraction to Hippolyte.

There may be just the faintest, unspoken intimation of a covert illicit love affair, but it is this that stirs Phèdre's indignation and so initiates her moral restoration after her short-lived acquiescence in deceit, incest and murder (1270). She understands Oenone's suggestion only too well and rejects it with utmost vehemence (1307-8). She once more gives free rein to her grievances at the erstwhile "chère Oenone" conveniently glossing over the fact that she was at all times free to reject the latter's well-meant though ill-fated advice. As she decides to take her fate into her own hands (1318) in an unmistakable echo of her Greek model's "I will arrange all well" (*Hipp* 709), she drives the poor servant away as a "monstre exécrable" and calls down the wrath of heaven upon her (1319-20: *Hipp* 683-84).

What follows is somewhat unexpected: Phèdre's indictment of her Nurse turns into fuming vociferations against the flattering advisers who encourage princes and kings to follow their evil proclivities (1320-26). This, we know, was a commonplace in Western drama in the days of absolutism. Tragedy was supposed to deal with the deeds of aristocratic and royal characters. As Maravall argued in *La cultura del barroco*, drama, like all other arts, was an instrument of propaganda for the dominant ideology. In baroque drama, from Lope de Vega to Corneille, royal persons had to be presented as terrestrial representatives of divine justice, entrusted with the task of maintaining or restoring order in society. Their evil deeds were to be ascribed to the influence of court flatterers and corrupt counsellors. Seneca's *Nutrix* had inveighed against the self-indulgence of the powerful and the wealthy who cannot rest satisfied with their fair share of things (*Phaed* 213-15). Racine reversed the message so as to comply with the conventions and constraints of his own day. Phèdre's concluding words may indeed appear, in the words of Maurice Delcroix, as "a lapse in Racine's tragic concentration" (203). But on another level of interpretation, we should not dismiss the possibility that the playwright intended such unwarranted generalities as evidence of continuing disorder in the Queen's sickly mind. This throws retrospective light on her hysterical condemnation of Oenone. Indeed, the genuine pathos in the latter's wistful parting words —

> Ah! dieux! pour la servir j'ai tout fait, tout quitté,
> Et j'en reçois ce prix? Je l'ai bien mérité
>
> (1327-28)

— does invite us to a reconsideration of her moral character and its dramatic function.

Commenting on this, Oenone's last appearance on-stage, Gordon Pocock asserts that "There is a level in *Phèdre* — an important level — at which it is pointless to try to argue about the relationship of the characters as if they were real people. At this level, Oenone is not just Phèdre's confidante — she represents the opportunistic Phèdre who is in complicity with her passion, and which the tormented Phèdre can both make use of and repudiate" (255). There is a well-known liking in current hermeneutics for reinterpreting masterpieces of the past in terms of myth and symbol. It is useful, however, to remember Coleridge's insight that a symbol "always partakes of the Reality which it renders intelligible" (30). A dramatic character can only be truly symbolic (as distinct from allegorical) in so far as it is "realistic" as well. It is true that Oenone's evolution seems to run more or less parallel to that of Phèdre: both are filled with revulsion and despair (266) at the mere thought of the Queen's dangerous love; after Thésée's alleged death Oenone tries to fulfil Phèdre's wishes when she argues that such love is no longer unlawful and advises her to meet Hippolyte; she alleviates Phèdre's fears for her "honour" when she concocts the slanderous scheme after Thésée's return; and she once more seeks to gratify the Queen's still burning passion (1266) when she advises her to come to terms with the weakness of human nature (1297-302). In all this, this humble woman may indeed be regarded as an accomplice, and therefore a symbol, of Phèdre's lawless cravings. But this by no means implies that she is merely one of those Racinian confidants whom Bowra described as mere "extensions of the chief characters, reflections of their desperate devices and instruments of their unconscious purposes" (26-27).

Phèdre's overwhelming presence and enduring fascination have led critics, producers and performers alike to concur with Jean Dubu's assertion that "despite the author's craftsmanship, the other characters look thin; even, at times, sound hollow" (224). Yet Oenone (who is not even mentioned by name in Dubu's essay) cannot in any way be looked down upon as a flat character: she has a consistent moral life of her own as well as the attending scruples and inner conflicts. Throughout I, iii, she adheres to the judgment of Phèdre's conscience (265-66); she repeatedly prods the Queen to desist from her ill-fated course (753-58,

773-80, 825-26, 869-83), and she voices a definite sense of transgression when she sets out to disclose the slanderous scheme: "Tremblante comme vous, j'en sens quelque remords" (906). True, this probably vicarious morality is all she has inherited from the Senecan Nurse's stern statement on virtue and the sanctions of crime (*Phaed* 128-77). This prompted Donald N. Levin to describe her as "morally purblind" (62) and to speak of "her usual faulty vision" (61). It is, however, erroneous to claim, as Pocock does, that Oenone "unhesitatingly" advises her patron to indulge her passion (260), or to insist with Weinberg that her "character is constructed in terms of a complete lack of moral scruples" (286).

The traditionally negative appraisal of Oenone derives from two main sources. One is Phèdre's pronouncements in the last two Acts of the play; but these highlight the Queen's closing in on her own subjective emotions and the concomitant decline of her mental sanity and moral integrity. The other is Racine's own comment on the "baseness" suitable to a lowly servant's character. Actually the word *bassesse* refers simultaneously to the moral vileness of the calumny and to the lowliness of the Nurse's social condition. What the text tells us is that while Oenone does not share Phèdre's exacting ideals, she is by no means deprived of any moral sense. Her scale of values is determined by the conventional sociology that prevailed in French classical theory as it did in the days of Euripides and Seneca: a menial character was not supposed to entertain the lofty principles to which "noble" personages were allegedly addicted. As Racine insists, Oenone is endowed, like her ancient models, with a servant's most prized virtue: total devotion to her mistress's life, honour and happiness — in that order. But she has a specificity of her own. Whereas both the Greek and Latin nurses abandon at an early stage their attempts at reminding the Queen of her duty, until Thésée's return Oenone strives to keep Phèdre's feelings and conduct within the bounds of common morality. Her first real lapse, the calumny, is made inevitable because the fruitless declaration and the King's return have created a situation in which Phèdre's honour and life are both threatened. In IV, vi she lapses for the second and last time, but the suggestion that the Queen should assume her sinful passion is offered half-heartedly and as a desperate last resource: in *Hippolutos* the Nurse was more crudely persuasive when she intimated that Theseus might follow the example of the many wise men who see with averted eyes their wives turned faithless (*Hipp*

462-65). Above all, Oenone's "remorse" (895) at her own proposal is enough evidence that she is aware of infringing her own code.

Racine's purpose in having the false accusation conceived and delivered by the Nurse was, he tells us in his Preface, to make the eponymous heroine "*un peu* moins odieuse" (italics added), but certainly not "tout à fait innocente". Nevertheless, Phèdre's irate revulsion at the Nurse's implicitly lewd proposal should not be taken to show that she has totally recovered her moral control. Faced as she now is with the dread consequences of the shameful slander, the dishonour inflicted upon the Prince and his probable death, faced, too, with awareness of her own share of responsibility in the whole tragic process, she desperately seeks a scapegoat to alleviate her self-condemnation. Her description of the once trusted confidante as a "monstre exécrable" is bound to remind us that Hippolyte himself once appeared as "un monstre effroyable" to her fickle eyes. But her indictment of Oenone has been prepared for, as Julian White pointed out, ever since she turned on the servant for the first time in III, i. The gradual worsening of her image of the Nurse runs parallel with her own steady moral deterioration. As she now regains control over herself in connection with Hippolyte's honour and life and with her own virtuous behaviour, she certainly stoops lower than ever in her craven outburst against a defenceless servant. Her vehement condemnation of Oenone is an unwarranted display of blind ungratefulness: it is surprising that so many commentators fail to perceive the essential unfairness, indeed the dishonesty that is here at work.

The mournful self-irony in the poor woman's parting lines reflects her despairing awareness of this change in Phèdre. Her suicide, which is almost simultaneous with Hippolyte's death, testifies to the intensity of her attachment to the most cherished of her moral values, the Queen's confidence, affection and esteem. Oenone dies a victim of Phèdre's malignant ungratefulness.

When Seneca's Phaedra appears onstage for her final confession, she is in a state of conspicuous distractedness (*Phaed* 1154-58). Nevertheless, while her last speech is couched in somewhat disorderly terms, it clearly broaches on two main themes: her continued passion for Hippolytus and her sense of guilt, both for the young man's death and the slighting of her husband's honour. She stabs herself in a mixed frenzy of frustration and remorse. Racine's Phèdre, too, is in deep confusion after her angry outburst at Oenone, but this is simply reported by her servant Panope in V, v. Phèdre herself remains off-stage throughout the first six scenes of Act V. When she reappears she is more composed than we have ever seen her. She may not have overheard Théramène's last words, where he describes her as Hippolyte's "mortal enemy" (1593). At any rate, she does not react to them any more than she does when Thésée hails her with sarcastic resentment: "Eh! bien vous triomphez, et mon fils est sans vie" (1594).

In both plays, the Queen at this point seems to be safe. The Latin Theseus does not even suspect his wife's responsibility for the death of his son. With greater psychological subtlety and credibility Racine has his Thésée repress his premonitory misgivings (1455-56) and vague suspicions (1481-82); he makes a pretence of accepting Oenone's version, in which he believes Phèdre concurs: "Je le crois criminel, puisque vous l'accusez" (1600). In what seems to be an ultimate echo of Euripides, he deliberately refuses to seek "d'odieuses lumières" which might only increase his misery (1602-604); and while vituperating the gods' "murderous gifts", he blames himself for the tragic loss of Hippolyte.

Phèdre's abrupt denial ("Non, Thésée", 1617) must be as startling as was Phaedra's even more explicit incipit, "Me, me ... invade" (*Phaed* 1159-60). But the substance of her 26-line speech and the manner of her delivery are in marked contrast with the Senecan 42-line expostulation. Both heroines return in order to vindicate the Prince, to make a public confession and to seek death. There is no dearth of Senecan echoes in the French play, but the substance and neat organization of Phèdre's final rhesis are entirely Racine's. Here again, close comparison of both texts should provide useful indications as to the specificity of his message.

It is first to be noted that the French playwright refrained from exploiting one of the two main motifs in the Latin Phaedra's confession: her continued love for her stepson. Phèdre certainly does not kill herself in any "metaphysical" expectation that she will somehow join her beloved in some other world beyond death (cf. *Phaed* 1179-80). In retrospect it appears indeed that her fiery passion has been eroding gradually under the pressure of her disillusionment and of the outward threats to which she is exposed. It was last mentioned — as "l'ardeur dont je suis embrasée" (846) — when she voiced her fear lest the Prince might denounce her to his father; it was later described as a "feu mal étouffé" (1194) which only jealousy has reactivated: "je brûle encore" (1266). It was not possessive yearning that was in the foreground of her mind in IV, vi, but moral indignation prompted by an overwhelming concern with Hippolyte's life and reputation endangered by the calumny. It is this sense of justice that now actuates her. By thus eliminating any suggestion of lasting emotional involvement, Racine achieves greater ethical concentration than did Seneca: nothing interferes with the two motives for Phèdre's repentance, the lawless passion and the appalling slander that she must expiate. Paradoxically, this purified motivation turns the French tragedy into a more convincing illustration than the Latin play of the inner workings of the moral conscience as preached by the Senecan *Nutrix*. As Weinberg cogently observed, "Racine thus endows his heroine with ... high moral dignity" (283).

Phèdre's speech can be broken down into two sections dealing respectively with responsibility (1623-32) and with punishment (1633-44).

The Queen first proclaims her stepson's innocence (1618-19) and takes the blame upon herself:

> C'est moi qui sur ce fils chaste et respectueux
> Osai jeter un oeil profane, incestueux.
>
> (1623-24)

Phaedra had likewise described Hippolytus as "juvenis castus", "pudicus, insons" (*Phaed* 1195-96), but whereas she had admitted from the start that she was the one who deserved punishment (*Phaed* 1159-60), she did not become specific until the end of her speech, when she acknowledged that she had slanderously accused the Prince of the very crime that her heart had conceived (*Phaed* 1192-94).

More important, Phaedra did not so much as mention Venus — who had been a handy excuse when she was trying to influence her Nurse — or the Nurse herself, who had initiated the slanderous device. Racine's Phèdre, on the contrary, apportions equal shares of responsibility; after declaring her guilt ("C'est moi"), she goes on:

> Le ciel mit dans mon sein une flamme funeste;
> La détestable Oenone a conduit tout le reste.
>
> (1625-26)

After this terse summary she embarks on a 6-line *narratio* that details the role allegedly played by Oenone:

> Elle a craint qu'Hippolyte, instruit de ma fureur,
> Ne découvrît un feu qui lui faisait horreur
> La perfide, abusant de ma faiblesse extrême,
> S'est hâtée à vos yeux de l'accuser lui-même.
> Elle s'en est punie, et fuyant mon courroux,
> A cherché dans les flots un supplice trop doux.
>
> (1624-32)

This passage has predictably been a source of considerable critical embarrassment. The debate is whether it represents what Maurice Delcroix called "un juste historique du crime" (208), a truthful objective abstract of the facts, or, in Bernard Weinberg's words, Phèdre's subjective "estimate of the respective responsibilities" (286). The text offers no reason for doubting her sincerity, but her veracity is certainly dubious. While her account is true to the outward facts of the story, her description of Oenone's character and motivations is obviously biased: when Phèdre uses such epithets as "detestable" and "perfidious", when she blames the Nurse for taking unfair advantage ("abusant") of her own feebleness, subjective appraisal obtrudes itself; the phrasing conveys a negative image of Oenone's character that we know to be distorted because it overlooks the woman's selfless goodwill and utter devotion; furthermore, Phèdre conveniently glosses over the fact that Oenone never acted without her own express authorization. Commenting on this passage, Federico Orlando rightly emphasizes "the enormous injustice and ingratitude that Phèdre shows Oenone" (48-49). In her posthumous smearing of Oenone's character she appears to be re-enacting the humble Nurse's scheming, but in a rancorous mood of unwarranted resentment. She is sincere, however. She will have no time to realize the nature of this infamy or to regain moral control as she was wont to do after previous lapses. All this constitutes evidence that evil has taken the upper hand in her, even though the pathos of her situation and the eloquence of her straightforwardness has deluded many critics into taking her interpretation of Oenone's character at face value.

The glaring untruth in Phèdre's final characterization of the Nurse is only one aspect of a wider web of contradictions. By any rational standards her ascription of responsibility for her incestuous longings to "le ciel", and to Oenone for the false accusation, exonerates the Queen of the guilt she had first taken upon herself. Nevertheless, in the second section of the speech she turns to her impending death which is assumed to be the correct punishment for her crimes.

In a transparent allusion to the Senecan version she first declares that she would have stabbed herself at an earlier moment — "Le fer aurait déjà tranché ma destinée" (1633) — were it not for the need to restore her stepson's reputation, which is now implicitly presented as a metonymy for virtue as such: "Mais je laissais gémir la vertu soupçonnée" (1634). Phèdre's absolute use of "*la* vertu" (instead of "*sa* vertu") offers an inverted image of the Nurse's similar shift from particular to general in III, iii: while the old woman had advocated sacrificing "tout, et même la vertu" (908) to the preservation of the Queen's life and reputation, Phèdre herself is now determined to sacrifice both her life and her reputation to the restoration of the Prince's virtuous repute. It was in order to give herself time for a public confession (Cf. *Phaed* 1191: "Audite, Athenae") that she resolved in favour of a slower death by poison:

> J'ai voulu, devant vous exposant mes remords,
> Par un chemin plus lent descendre chez les morts.
> (1635-36)

With consummate craftsmanship Racine thus manages to account for his departing from the Senecan pattern. In the eyes of a French seventeenth-century audience it would of course have been a breach of decorum to have Phèdre stab herself on the stage. Furthermore, the Latin Phaedra's confession and suicide signalled a change of mind that was totally unprepared for, except perhaps as the materialization of the Nurse's prophecy that she could not expect to eschew the judgment of her conscience. The French Phèdre's decision ("J'ai voulu"), on the contrary, appears as the outcome of a psychological process that was initiated when she resolved to take her fate in her own hands (1318).

Here too, however, despite her obvious assurance that she is doing the right thing, there is uncontrovertible though unobtrusive evidence of delusion and mental confusion. This is first underscored by her ambivalent mention of "heaven": "Le ciel" which lit a baleful fire in her heart in line 1625 can hardly be the same as "le ciel" to which her very existence is as much an outrage as it is to her husband (1642). The former, obviously, is the abode of Venus, the realm of darkness, a poetic image for the objectionable impulses to which she has been increasingly yielding; the latter is the abode of the Sun, the realm of light and retributive justice, a poetic image for the purity of virtue and the stern demands of righteousness. That the same word should be used simply reflects her confused sense that she has been a battlefield for a conflict between forces that are beyond her control to an equal degree, simultaneously impelling her towards lawless passion and towards merciless self-indictment.

The confusion in Phèdre's mind between "ciel" as transcendent heaven and "ciel" as terrestrial sky compels us to question the tone of certainty in her parting lines:

> Et la mort, à mes yeux dérobant la clarté,
> Rend au jour qu'ils souillaient toute sa pureté.
>
> (1643-44)

In an implicit paraphrase of the Latin Phaedra's *quod vivo*, Phèdre experiences her very being as a stain defiling the bright purity of the world, a stain that her self-annihilation will wipe out, she trusts, thus restoring the purity of the world. What the play as a whole tells us, however, is that the Queen's disappearance cannot restore the purity of the world for the simple reason that the world has never been pure in the first place. None of the major characters can be regarded as blameless. We should not miss the irony implicit in Hippolyte's bland assertion, "Le jour n'est pas plus pur que le fond de mon coeur" (1112), which so closely anticipates Phèdre's last words: after all, in loving Aricie he transgresses the express will of the King, his father. Even Aricie, immaculate though she may seem to be, comes as near as she can to denouncing the Queen, despite Hippolyte's injunction (cf. 1347-50 and 1445-46). Above all, Thésée's inveterate skirt-chasing has been fully documented in the very first scene of the play. When Phèdre's tragedy is viewed in the complex totality of the work, it becomes apparent that she is singled out by a utopian idealism, a refusal to come to terms with the basic impurity of human nature, which are entirely foreign to her husband.

Seneca's play ends with an inordinately protracted lament by Theseus on the loss of his son. Only the last two lines are devoted to his dead wife:

> Istam terra defossam premat
> gravisque tellus impio capiti incubet.
>
> (1279-80)

Racine discarded this contemptuous curse. His Thésée's obituary words express with equal terseness a revealing sense of puzzled helplessness:

> D'une action si noire,
> Que ne peut avec elle expirer la mémoire!
> (1645-46)

As far as I know, Francesco Orlando is the only commentator to have given due attention to this passage, which is in fact the climactic appearance of a recurrent microstructure. In his psychoanalytical interpretation, this is a choice example of Freudian negation (*Verneinung*), a mental operation in which we explicitly negate ideas, affects or deeds that we in fact wish to repress from our conscious minds.

Crowning as it does a sequence of four earlier occurrences,[4] Thésée's pronouncement deserves all the more scrutiny as it also conveys the final appraisal uttered by the highest-ranking person in the play. It is couched in a mode of disillusioned wistfulness ("Que ne peut ...?") which is in stark contrast not only with the loathing voiced by Seneca's Theseus but also with the corresponding utterance in Euripides' *Hippolutos*, where the goddess Artemis announces that she will not allow Phaidra's love to sink into oblivion unsung (*Hipp* 1430).

It would be idle to speculate on Euripides' motives for declaring worthy of celebration the story of a woman whose career he had just described as a miserable failure in all respects. A more relevant comparison is with the conclusion of Lope's *El castigo sin venganza*: the

---

[4] As conveniently listed by Orlando (110-11), these refer: to Thésée's erotic exploits –

> Hipp.: Heureux si j'avais pu ravir à la mémoire
> Cette indigne moitié d'une si belle histoire!
> (93-94)

– to Pasiphaé's unnatural love for a bull, –

> Oe.: Oublions-les, Madame. Et qu'à tout l'avenir
> Un silence éternel cache ce souvenir.
> (251-52)

– to Phèdre's love confession, –

> Ph.:   qu'en un profond oubli
> Cet horrible secret demeure enseveli
> (719-20)

– and to her incestuous passion itself, –

> Hipp.: Oubliez, s'il se peut, que je vous ai parlé,
> Madame, et que jamais une bouche si pure
> Ne s'ouvre pour conter cette horrible aventure.
> (1347-49)

gracioso addresses the audience as if it were a law court ("senado") and claims that the Ferrarese tragedy, which had struck Italy with awed amazement ("asombro"), is now an "ejemplo" for Spain. This should by no means be regarded as a facile contrivance for closure. On the contrary, Batín's words provide a major key to the function of the play, which is fully consonant with the didactic essence of baroque drama. What he calls "this tragedy" is exemplary in two ways. Firstly, through Federico and Casandra it fulfils the edifying purpose of the Phaedra syndrome as a cautionary tale targeted at young people's proclivity to yield to sexual impulse regardless of social norms, natural law and divine commands. Secondly, in the person of the Duke of Ferrara, it extols the righteous behaviour of the good ruler who restores order in his dominions and, in administering justice, rises above both his fatherly love and the legitimate anger of his slighted honour.

We can understand that Thésée's shallow mind should be steeped in confusion: all he can do is wish that the appalling events might vanish from human memory. An attentive audience, however, may well wonder why Racine should have him utter such a trite indictment immediately after Phèdre has restored his son's honour, acknowledged her share of guilt, atoned for her crimes and protested her fundamental innocence. Conceivably it would have been easy for the writer to devise some more constructive conclusion, analogous to Batín's in Lope's play and more consonant with the traditional cautionary import of the legend. Indeed, if we are to believe Racine's brother Louis, no less an authority than Antoine Arnauld himself, the most prominent exponent of Jansenist radicalism, suggested just this type of conclusion:

> Il n'y a rien à reprendre au caractère de Phèdre, puisque par ce caractère [Racine] nous donne cette grande leçon, que lorsqu'en punition de fautes précédentes, Dieu nous abandonne à nous-mêmes et à la perversité de notre coeur, il n'est point d'excès où nous ne puissions nous porter, même en les détestant.[5]

The recurrence of the repression/negation/suppression pattern and its climactic appearance at the end of the play should perhaps be taken as an intimation that Thésée's final words reflect some preoccupation more deeply rooted in the writer's own mind. If Thésée is right in assuming that the memory of the "action si noire" will, *unfortunately*, outlive its heroine, one reason may be that Racine himself, by writing this play, has powerfully contributed to keeping the tale alive — and wishes he hadn't. Why?

---

[5] Quoted in Picard ed. 1951, I, 67-68.

6

PHÈDRE, RACINE AND THE ANGUISH OF THE TIMES

A work of dramatic art worthy of the supreme form of canonization that has befallen *Phèdre* cannot be merely a self-referential artefact as a fading school of literary theorists have claimed in recent decades.[1] Despite the critical consensus that Racine's tragedy deals with the perennial problem of good and evil, of innocence and guilt, a variety of interpretations has been proffered in the course of the centuries as generations of critics reassessed its significance. To be sure, authors and critics are subject to the prevailing *Weltanschauung* or dominant ideology of their times. That the play survived and indeed gained in depth and attractiveness throughout this process testifies to its inherent polysemic scope. Our perception of the real world, too, is constantly being revised and refined as the progress of experience and knowledge enables us to view it from ever new angles with ever more sophisticated instruments. Undoubtedly Racine created what Robert Alter in *The Pleasures of Reading* recently described as "a persuasive representation of reality", discussion of which will never come to an end. I propose to illustrate this process of enduring revaluation by attempting to clarify the status of the more unreal characters in the play: the metaphysical, metadiegetic entities that constantly influence characters and plot although they never appear on-stage and have therefore only inferential existence for the audience — the gods and goddesses and other mythological supernatural beings that French analysts like to lump together as "le mythe" or "le sacré". This problem should be approached from three different angles encompassing the three discrete viewpoints of the central character, of the writer himself and the contemporary audience, and of the later audiences and critics that have submitted to the unending fascination of this tragedy.

---

[1] A wondrously post-modern discussion will be found in Danielle and David Kaisergruber and Jacques Lampert, *"Phèdre" de Racine* (1972).

Reading the play as a self-contained whole, there can be no denying that Racine's heroine — like Euripides' and unlike Seneca's — really believes in the actual existence and intervention of Venus and the other mythical beings that play such an important part in her speculations and, as she assumes, her life. That much was implied in the playwright's choice of an ancient Greek story in order to materialize on the stage the old Socratic problem of correct knowledge versus evil behaviour. Phèdre cannot account for her tragic plight in terms other than those of her own culture — at least as it could be perceived or imagined by Racine.

It is not necessary to insist that neither Racine nor his contemporaries entertained any belief in the actual existence of pagan deities. In seventeenth-century writing these could only be awarded ornamental or metaphorical status. They symbolized experiences pertaining to the Christian world-view. Medieval authors could ascribe a sinner's evil proclivities to the workings of Satan, but the Renaissance had rendered such characters obsolete to many, though they remained operational in such works as the Spanish *auto sacramental*, Jesuit drama, Milton's epic and some plays by Vondel or Gryphius. At the same time, the Reformation, the Counter-Reformation and the ensuing movements of Western theological thought had generated new, more internalized, more spiritualized and more diversified conceptions of the faith. The dramatic function of the classical-pagan setting now fashionable was to give a local habitation and a name to the inward experiences and preoccupations formerly impersonated by the devils and saints of miracle plays and moralities. The message of *Phèdre* accordingly has constantly been interpreted in terms of Christian theodicy and ethics.

In order to approximate as closely as possible what is likely to have been in Racine's mind when he composed his crowning masterpiece, however, it is not enough to remember the general Christian background of Western culture at the time. For in the aftermath of Luther and of the Council of Trent, the impact of Calvin and Jansenius had spread among the Western intelligentsia a more radical form of Christianity which involved a definite return to the pessimistic determinism of St Augustine. Whether in its Protestant or Catholic versions, this doctrine emphasized the omnipotence of God and belittled the efficacy of the human will. It asserted predestination. The only way to salvation was through divine grace. Man's impotence in repressing evil impulses was taken to result from God's withholding of his grace. Phèdre is unable to crush her sinful longings despite her fundamental innocence and the clarity of her moral judgment. In terms of Christian thought, the alleged power of Venus is a symbolic mode of illustrating the corrupt nature of man and woman when God refuses to favour them with his redeeming grace and leaves them prey to the essential corruption allegedly induced by our first parents' original sin.

There is much to commend interpretations that rely on our knowledge of the dominant ideology in Racine's own circles. In defining Phèdre as an innocent person "à qui la grâce a manqué" — a view derided by Voltaire in 1760, but still maintained by Jules Lemaître in 1908 (62) — they posit the likely hypothesis that the pantheon in the play should be regarded as a metaphor for the stern deity of radical Christian theology in its French form, Jansenism. This interpretation was given its most elaborate formulation in Lucien Goldmann's *Le Dieu caché* (1956).

The notion that Racine intended his heroine to be doomed for eternity despite the manifest element of innocence in her character and her obdurate determination to resist temptation is utterly repellent to the modern mind. Nevertheless, Voltaire's mockery of current interpretative commonplaces failed to encourage any sustained attempt at reappraisal until the end of the nineteenth century when Gustave Lanson in his epochal *Histoire de la littérature française* (1894) offered an optimistic vision of Phèdre "se rachetant par la confession publique et la mort volontaire" (547). The idea that the play's ending was meant to illustrate a syncretic, "baroque" restoration of cosmic order that included spiritual salvation for the protagonist made it more consonant to our humane sense of divine justice. Half a century after Lanson, Georges Poulet suggested that Phèdre, because of her acceptance of her guilt and punishment might be "une chrétienne à qui la grâce *n'a pas manqué*" (150), and Ivan Barko cleverly handled the darkness and light imagery in the play to turn her into a Christ figure who sacrifices her life in order to save the world. Actually, the play offers no direct indication that the dying Phèdre is seeking or expecting any sort of salvation in the Christian sense of the term or that her death will, as she hopes, purify the world. The only things *she* knows is that she is now bound to appear before the tribunal of Minos, and there is no evidence that the "pardon" (1289) for which she craved is likely to be granted.

A new, highly unorthodox prospect opened up when Leo Spitzer in his notable essay on "Le Récit de Théramène" ventured the idea that *Phèdre* "amounts to an accusation of the world order and invites man's revolt against the gods" (93). A few years later Michel Butor went so far as to claim that one of the main themes of the tragedy is "la haine des dieux, ou si l'on préfère, le blasphème" (29). And Roland Barthes envisioned the whole of Racinian tragedy as "essentiellement procès de Dieu" (48). Negative assessments of the gods' interference in human affairs do indeed permeate the play. Phèdre is repeatedly driven by her sense of her own innocence to shift responsibility for her criminal passion onto the supernatural beings who, she feels, control her nature and fate. She views herself as an "objet infortuné des vengeances célestes" and she unequivocally revolts against

> ces dieux qui dans mon flanc
> Ont allumé le feu fatal à tout mon sang;
> Ces dieux qui se sont fait une gloire cruelle
> De séduire le coeur d'une faible mortelle.
>
> (677-82)

She beseeches Minos to pardon her because she is not responsible for "crimes" to which she has been prompted by "un dieu cruel" (1289). Thésée, too, vituperates the gods for their "murderous favours" (1613), their "baleful kindness" (1615), their perfidious implementing of his mistaken condemnation of Hippolyte: "Inexorables dieux, qui m'avez trop servi!" (1572). Even Aricie sadly blames the gods rather than Phèdre or Thésée for the death of her lover: "Par un triste regard elle accuse les dieux" (1584). The Prince's atrocious death itself casts ironic retrospective light on his immature assumption that "l'innocence n'a rien à redouter" (996) and on his starry-eyed confidence in "l'équité des dieux" (1351). Not until he is facing death does the blasphemous truth dawn upon him: "Le ciel, dit-il, m'arrache une innocente vie" (1561).

The consensus among the characters in *Phèdre* represents the climax of a trend which, as several critics have shown in recent decades, was present in Racine's drama from the outset. Few of its tragic characters fail to denounce or deplore the injustice and the sadistic cruelty of "the gods":

> Voilà de ces grands Dieux la suprême justice!
> Jusques au bord du crime ils conduisent nos pas;

> Ils nous le font commettre, et ne l'excusent pas!
> Prennent-ils donc plaisir à faire des coupables,
> Afin d'en faire après d'illustres misérables?
>
> *(La Thébaïde* [1664], III, ii)
>
> Je ne sais de tout temps quelle injuste puissance
> Laisse le crime en paix et poursuit l'innocence.
> De quelque part sur moi que je tourne les yeux,
> Je ne vois que malheurs qui condamnent les Dieux.
>
> *(Andromaque* [1670], III. i)

Such coherence and continuity suggest that a literary motif that may have started as a harmless conventional indictment of pagan gods increasingly turned out to reflect a deeper preoccupation in the author's mind: his growing obsession with the fundamental contradiction in Christian theology, especially in its radical form, between the conception of a transcendent godhead that is all-knowing, all-powerful and supremely benevolent on one hand, and the uncontrovertible evidence of undeserved suffering in this world and horrific prospects of undeserved doom after death on the other.

In rational logic this is the aporia which Pierre Bayle was to formulate a quarter of a century later in his *Réponses aux questions d'un provincial*: if God, he said,

> a prévu le péché d'Adam, et qu'il n'ait pas pris des mesures très certaines pour le détourner, il manque de bonne volonté pour l'homme ... S'il a fait tout ce qu'il a pu pour empêcher la chute de l'homme, et qu'il n'ait pu en venir à bout, il n'est donc pas tout puissant, comme nous le supposions.

Reasoning from which it is to be inferred that

> La manière dont le mal s'est introduit sous l'empire d'un être infiniment bon, infiniment saint, infiniment puissant est non seulement inexplicable, mais même incompréhensible.[2]

There are only two ways out of this conundrum. One is to impugn the Christian definition of the divine attributes, which is what the characters in *Phèdre* do when they tax the gods with cruelty. But Racine was undoubtedly a devout Christian. It is almost ludicrous to fancy

---

[2] Quoted in Delumeau, 282. It is relevant to note that this unimpeachable logic did not shake Bayle's faith. Such reasonings, he argued, make man aware of "sa ténèbre et son impuissance, et la nécessité d'une autre révélation". And shortly before his death he declared: "Je meurs en philosophe chrétien, pénétré et persuadé des bontés et de la miséricorde de Dieu" (*ibid.*).

that he could have consciously entertained, even in a symbolic way, such blasphemous denial of the accepted "revealed" truths about God's attributes and his infinite benevolence in any of his writings. Jean Dubu offered a more plausible diagnosis of the relationship between play and playwright than did Spitzer, Butor and Barthes when he pointed to the "contradiction ... between [Racine's] own metaphysical beliefs and those that his heroes illustrated on the stage". Dubu put forward the proposition that Racine's retirement from the stage after *Phèdre* must have resulted from his "disquiet at the incompatibility of [these] two metaphysical worlds, realizing that to certain people they may appear to be equated, and recoiling before the ambiguity he has thus expressed". This is indeed the artist's peculiar aporia. His imagination, as Keats noted, "has as much delight in conceiving an Iago as an Imogen" (227), but if his genius can make them convincingly come alive, reader and audience are tempted to identify him with his creatures, especially when they utter statements that may be construed as an outlet for or a projection of views that his conscious mind would in fact negate or repress.

The other way out of Bayle's dilemma had been offered in the 1690s by Bossuet in his *Traité de la concupiscence*:

> C'est encore s'abandonner à cette concupiscence que saint Jean réprouve, que d'apporter des yeux curieux a la recherche des choses divines ou des mystères de la religion ... La foi et l'humilité sont les seules guides qu'il faut suivre ...: combien ont trouvé leur perte dans la trop grande méditation des secrets de la predestination et de la grace! ... Que sert de rechercher curieusement les moyens de concilier nostre liberté avec les decrets de Dieu? N'est ce pas assez de scavoir que Dieu qui l'a faite la scait mouvoir et la conduire a ses fins cachées sans la détruire? Prions le donc de nous diriger dans la voye du salut et de se rendre maistre de nos desirs par les moyens qu'il scait (26).

The Bishop of Meaux was no follower of Jansenius. Die-hard Jansenists would be even more categorical in condemning any attempt at justifying, fathoming, questioning, much less blaming, the ways of God to man. Bossuet's almost naive casuistry about a will that is controlled from above yet remains free gives the game away: when rational thinking points to the "inexplicable and even incomprehensible" contradictions in the dogma, the pious should seek salvation in abdicating rationality.

The supremacy of faith over reason was a traditional tenet of traditional theology. At the close of the seventeenth century orthodox

Christian thinkers lay special emphasis on the faithful's duty to discard rational logic based on experience when it clashes with Revelation. This appears nowadays to have been a rear-guard battle or, better still, a flight reflex, a *Verneinung*, which highlights an intriguing homology between Phèdre's suicide, Racine's temporary renouncing of his craft and the mood of part of the Christian intelligentsia as the Western world stood on the threshold of the age of unbelief.

Phèdre's self-poisoning is an escape from life, conscience and consciousness: she is unable to come to terms with the anguished confusion created by her dual sense of guilt and innocence. And Racine sought safety from blasphemous temptations (and, probably, from public odium as well) in a twelve-year silence which, as Philip Butler observed "looks more like a mutilation than an achievement" (1974, 89). In an extraordinary feat of brinkmanship he had symbolically unburdened himself of unacceptable misgivings about divine providence through the impious utterances of his characters. His last tragedy of classical inspiration offered such a convincing portrayal of metaphysical and ethical ambiguity that the play could be regarded as a scandalous source of temptation: Thésée is his mouthpiece when he expresses the wish that the story itself might vanish from human memory. This, we may conjecture, was one of the reasons why Racine chose to desist from the potential hubris of probing the murkier depths of human experience and questioning divine justice. His correspondence offers clear indications that he sought (and found) spiritual repose in what he himself described, in a letter to Madame de Maintenon, as "childlike submissiveness" to the decrees of the Roman church and in unquestioning adherence to the orthodox notion of divine providence. As he wrote to his son on 21 July 1698:

> il n'y a rien de si doux au monde que le repos de la conscience, et de regarder Dieu comme un père qui ne nous manquera pas dans tous nos besoins.[3]

The historical-biographical approach does much to clarify the significance of *Phèdre* for Racine's outlook and career. We need to have a close eye to the particular audience he intended writing for and to understand what he was writing in relation to that audience's assumptions and beliefs. Yet however satisfactory this may be to literary historians and academic analysts, it cannot account for the play's

---
[3] Quoted in Picard 1977, 46.

continued hold over readers, critics and theatre-goers through many succeeding generations. It is true that well into the twentieth century scholarly interpretations remained mostly within the frame-work of Christian beliefs and controversies, if only to enlist the playwright among those who blasphemously found it impossible to justify the ways of God to men. But since Racine's day belief in the supernatural has steadily been eroding under the impact of Enlightenment rationalism, scientific progress and the general rebellion against ethical imperatives allegedly decreed by God. Human behaviour is no longer accounted for by the workings of metaphysical agencies but in definitely this-worldly sociological, psychological and biological terms. What kind of sense can *Phèdre* make to a secular culture such as ours? Where does its lasting attraction reside for those outside the faith?

An unexpectedly early clue can be found in La Rochefoucauld's *Maximes*, which had reached print a dozen years before *Phèdre* was first performed. The interest of this work for my present purpose derives from the fact, underscored by A.J. Krailsheimer, that "there is virtually no mention of religion in the *Maximes*, and, more important, human conduct is condemned and praised in purely human terms" (95). Maxim 43 reads as follows:

> L'homme croit souvent se conduire, lorsqu'il est conduit, et pendant que par son esprit il tend à un but, son coeur l'entraîne insensiblement à un autre.

This aphorism offers a succinct prefigurement of Phèdre's plight. On several occasions the Queen voices her bewildered realization that she has been speaking, acting or desiring in spite of herself ("malgré moi"). It can be argued, using the rudimentary psychological terminology of the period, that her "esprit" (a term that denotes reason, moral conscience and conscious will) is overcome by her "coeur" (a word that coyly refers to the irrational urges of emotion and instinct, especially of a sexual nature). Such shifts occur "insensiblement", that is to say, in an involuntary and even unconscious manner, as if in a trance. La Rochefoucauld's phrasing for this baffling process, so contrary to the Socratic identification of correct knowledge and correct behaviour and to the notion of free will in mainstream Christian thought, strikingly anticipates Sigmund Freud's observation in *The Ego and the Id* to the effect that "what we call our ego behaves essentially passively in life, and that *we are 'lived'* by unknown and uncontrollable forces" (XIX, 23; italics added). The seat of these forces is the unconscious part of our selves. For the section of our unconscious mind that produces our so-called "lower", non-rational instincts and emotions, Freud used the word *das Es* (the id) which Georg Groddeck in *Das Buch vom Es* (1923) had borrowed from Nietsche. Whereas the ego, Freud asserted, "represents what we call reason and common sense ... the id contains the passions", and while "the functional importance of the ego is manifested in the fact that normally control over the approaches to motility [i.e. behaviour] devolves upon it" (*ibid.*), it is also a fact, which La Rochefoucauld had noted, that our rational self constantly carries into action the wishes of the id as if they were his own.

This is as apposite a description of Phèdre's sense of impotence and self-estrangement as was La Rochefoucauld's maxim. Not surprisingly. For, as Freud went on to note, "we all have impressions of the same kind". The scope may range from the chain-smoker's inability to shed his habit despite fear of cancer to Gladstone's inability to give up objectionable sexual practices despite fear of hell. It certainly encompasses Phèdre's inability to suppress her passion. Such a statement should not be taken to mean that Racine's heroine is liable to psychoanalysis: she is not a real person but a figment of the playwright's imagination, and she has no existence outside printed page or stage performance. We can only suggest that the concepts and the lexicon of psychoanalysis may supply an explanation of Phèdre's character and fate that can make sense to an audience for whom anthropomorphic deities endowed with intellect, will and power have become irrelevant myths. Although Racine's literary genius facilitates a willing suspension of disbelief, we cannot assume, as Phèdre does, that her sinful passion is due to a curse from a pagan goddess; nor can we interpret it, as Racine and his contemporaries did, as an unavoidable consequence of Original Sin; or claim, as did more radical theologians, that it is an unmistakable sign that God, in his inscrutable wisdom, had doomed her for eternity. In the this-worldly, man-centred approach already represented by La Rochefoucauld, Phèdre's compulsive urge can vaguely be ascribed to her "heart". In terms of present-day psychology, it originates in the erotic component of her id: we experience no difficulty in empathizing with a heroine who is unable to repress a powerful instinct that we know to be rooted in the biology of all living creatures.

While the function of Venus in the play can readily be decoded as figurative language for the operation of the sex drive in Phèdre's unconscious, it should be remembered that she is only one in the cast of Olympian or semi-Olympian beings who, significantly, never appear onstage although their alleged presence and influence pervade Phèdre's self-awareness. If, to borrow Freud's phrase about the spirits and demons of animistic societies in *Totem und Tabu*, Venus is "a result of [Phèdre's] tendency to project mental processes into the outside", a mere "projection" of her "emotional impulses" (XIX, 92), the same surely can be said of the other extra-terrestrials peopling the supernatural metatext that surrounds the tragedy with an aura of sacredness. Commentators tend to lump together Venus, the Sun, Neptune and Minos as constituents of a collective whole, an undifferenciated amalgam variously described as the metaphysical god, *deus absconditus*, myth or *le sacré*. Such a global approach, however, obliterates distinctions which can be highlighted by more refined hermeneutic methods. For while Venus, the Sun, Neptune and Minos are united in shared sacredness, closer examination of the text reveals that Racine, wittingly or unwittingly, assigned each of them a specific sphere of action. Each represents a discrete facet of the seemingly combined interference of the mythical pantheon. Two possible dividing lines come to mind. Venus, the Sun and Neptune are gods and have their abode in *le ciel*; Minos reigns in *les enfers*. Taken together they provide an objective correlative for the totality of the supernatural world. But a different taxonomy is more to the point: whereas Venus evidently impersonates the morally and socially objectionable impulses in Phèdre, the Sun and Minos are divine warrant for the higher ethical values to which her conscience adheres; Neptune stands apart with a status of puzzling complexity.

Solar imagery in *Phèdre* has received an almost confusing amount of interpretive attention in recent decades.[4] Its centrality is obvious from the heroine's very first appearance:

> Oe.: Vous vouliez vous montrer et revoir la lumière,
> Vous la voyez, Madame, et prête à vous cacher,
> Vous haïssez le jour que vous veniez chercher.
> Ph.: Noble et brillant auteur d'une triste famille,
> . . . . .
> Soleil, je te viens voir pour la dernière fois!
> (166-72)

---

[4] See notably Marc Eigeldinger's *La Mythologie solaire dans l'oeuvre de Racine*.

Most commentators have duly noted the twofold function of the mythical sun in *Phèdre*. Jean Starobinski's identification of the Sun with "l'oeil de Dieu", the "Regard absolu" of a "Juge transcendant" repeats Jules Lemaître's view that it calls up "l'idée de l'oeil de Dieu partout présent, partout ouvert sur notre conscience" (254). While Lucien Goldmann somewhat arbitrarily equated the Sun with Pascal's "hidden god" (352), there is a general consensus that Phèdre's Sun and the surrounding cluster of images involving day and night, light and darkness and the bright purity of the sky, are symbolic not only of godlike omniscience, but also of what J.D. Hubert, Ivan Barko, Odette de Mourgues and many others concur in describing as the perfection of the moral order. More specifically, the Sun as the source of light is a projection of Phèdre's own self-knowledge, which she fears to see shared. Her initial desire to "see the light" of day and "show herself" is immediately superseded, as she announces, by constant, recurrent revulsion: "Je voulais ... dérober au jour une flamme si noire" (309-10); "triste rebut de la nature entière,/Je me cachais au jour, je fuyais la lumière" (1241-42).

In Phèdre's mythical imagination there is no escape from omniscience: "Misérable! et je vis? et je soutiens la vue/De ce sacré soleil dont je suis descendue?" (1273-74). It is of course from her own consciousness that Phèdre cannot conceal her crimes. But while the Sun is a projection of her self-awareness, it is also a projection of her moral conscience. In the same breath as she voices her recoiling from the light of knowledge, she condemns her passion as a "dark flame" and a "crime". Throughout the play daylight is associated with the immaculate moral purity that her death, she trusts, will restore to the cosmos. To a Christian audience the phantasmatic sun-god is an adequate metaphor for the all-seeing deity from whose infallible judgment none can escape. But it is equally apposite as a projection of Phèdre's own self-knowledge and self-indictment.

In his controversial "psycho-critical" study of the play Charles Mauron surprisingly failed to point to the judicial function of the Sun. There is indeed an indisputable link between this function and the fact (emphasized by Mauron) that the Sun is one of the Queen's forbears. Racine, as we know, is here calling on the legend that Helios, father of Pasiphae, had disclosed Aphrodite's adulterous affair with Ares: in order to avenge herself the irate goddess had thrown a curse upon his daughter. In his capacity as Phèdre's grandfather the sun-god appears as an adequate figure of authority, the legitimate upholder of righteousness and the fountainhead of the assumptions underlying her ethical self-appraisal. It seems as if Racine had anticipated Freud's claim, in his enquiry about the origins of the super-ego, that "Religion, morality, and a social sense — the chief elements in the higher side of man — were ... acquired phylogenetically out of the father-complex" (XIX, 37). In this function, the role he plays in *le ciel* is complemented in *les enfers* by Phèdre's father, Minos.

From the beginning of the written tradition, and conceivably in the earlier oral tradition as well, an explicit link had been established between Phaidra's character and fate and her mother's. The Queen herself had constantly ascribed her devious sexual yearnings to the same curse that plagued her mother — a primitive "explanation" for the workings of heredity. Minos is absent from *Hippolutos*: Phaidra's ethical principles coincide with public opinion, with whose demands her suicide (as she believes) complies. In Seneca Phaedra's sense of higher values is traced to a *ratio* whose law she strenuously strives to dodge; it is her *Nutrix* who warns her that she had better be mindful of her ancestry and invites her to "remember [her] father" (*Phaed* 149-57). But when Racine's Hippolyte in the first Act describes his stepmother as "la fille *de Minos* et de Pasiphaé" (36), he is not merely uttering one of the most melodious lines in French literature: he informatively summarizes the Queen's dual heredity. As her mother's daughter she is submitted to the malevolence of Venus, but her acute sense of virtue and justice is a legacy she has inherited from her father. That Minos is the model to which she should strive to conform is stated in Act III, when Oenone ineffectually beseeches her to quench her flame and engage in political pursuits worthy of the daughter of Minos (955-56). Not until Act IV does Racine endow the latter with full significance, when Phèdre herself, struck with horror at her ignoble plot to dispose of Aricie, recoils from the merciless light of the Sun and thinks of seeking shelter in death and the darkness of hell ("la nuit infernale", 1237), only to remember that her own father sits there in stern judgment over the dead. In Seneca's play Minos is simply Phaedra's living father. As an image of rectitude and authority he obviously cuts a far more impressive figure in Racine, who takes him after he has been appointed one of the three judges in the Elysean fields.

The close collocation of Minos and the Sun in Phèdre's speech of IV, vi together with the visual imagery connected with both of them ("je soutiens la *vue*", 1272; "Mon père ... *verra* sa fille", 1282) coalesce to bring out their functional complementarity. The Sun (in sky-heaven and in life) and Minos (in hell and in death) are images of omniscience, absolute infallible judicial power and inescapable punishment. To Phèdre's mind they are real transcendent beings who know the truth about her as she herself knows it and who appraise her emotions, thoughts and deeds in the light of her own ethical principles. For the modern reader they are fictional external projections of her super-ego, the unconscious instance whose function, Freud wrote, is "in the form of conscience to exercise censorship over morals" (XIX, 37). Phèdre apprehends the similarity of her and her mother's fates as being equally due to Venus' curse. The text carries no indication that she might be aware of any organic link between Minos' righteousness and her principles. That the playwright had her project her moral conscience into the shapes of her father and grandfather is his own innovation. In this remarkable flash of psychological insight it is permissible to see a poetic anticipation of Freud's notion first expounded in *Zur Einführung des Narziszmus* (1914), that "the institution of conscience [is] at bottom an embodiment, first of parental criticism, and subsequently of that of society" (XIV, 96).

In her pathetic, hopeless appeal for her father's pardon, Phèdre exclaims: "Un dieu cruel a perdu ta famille" (1289). No editor it seems has bothered to inquire who this cruel male deity may be. John Cairncross boldly translates the line as "Venus' wrath has doomed your race" despite the lack of evidence for any transsexual leanings in the goddess of love. Unless we postulate some improbable slip of Racine's, we must admit that what he had in mind was a divine curse that was thrown not by Venus on Pasiphaé and her daughters, but by some male god on Minos and his breed. Indeed according to a story recounted by Strabo (X, 4, 8), Minos, in his bid for the throne of Crete had promised to sacrifice to Poseidon a bull of uncommon beauty that had come from the sea; he aroused the god's wrath by substituting an inferior animal; Poseidon took revenge for this outrage by afflicting Minos' wife with an outlandish sexual appetite for the bull. It is quite possible that Racine's "dieu cruel" is none other than Neptune, the "dieu vengeur" (1160) from whom Hippolyte's father expects "swift justice" (1190). His alleged cruelty at this point is somewhat unexpected for until then he had been surrounded with favourable connotations: not only has

Thésée turned to him to restore his slighted honour; Hippolyte too had earlier described him as a tutelary god who could be relied upon to protect Phèdre's husband (621-22).

Neptune does not reach the foreground of the Olympian metatext until we come to Théramène's report of the Prince's death. The famous "récit de Théramène" is certainly the passage in which the modern audience is most forcefully called upon to suspend disbelief. Nevertheless our pedestrian, naturalistic minds will find total plausibility in an account offered in the first century BC by Diodorus Siculus:

> Hippolytus, who was driving a chariot when he heard of [Phaedra's] accusation [against him] was so distraught in spirit that the horses got out of control and pulled him after them by the reins, and in the event the chariot was smashed to bits and the youth, becoming entangled in the leathern thongs, was dragged along till he died (IV, 62, 3).

Why did the French playwright choose to disregard this account and to preserve the two supernatural ingredients in the dramatic tradition: divine interference (Zeus in *Hippolutos*, Neptune in *Phaedra*) and the monster disgorged by the sea?

In his essay on the *récit* Leo Spitzer adduced two arguments in defence of the wildly improbable episode: on one hand, "In the ancient world, the monster had its legitimate place as one of the forces of nature"; on the other, "in the world of Christian values, the monstrous must appear as a threat to the cosmos, sent by *natura parens* to inflict death" (123). The latter claim is not very convincing. Actually the awesome circumstances surrounding the Prince's death are liable to a variety of symbolic interpretations "in the world of Christian values". Hippolyte could even conceivably be turned into a Christ figure, undeservedly sacrificed to enlighten and so redeem, his father. It is more likely that Racine stayed within the radical logic of predestination theology. Although Théramène at first disclaims any personal perception of divine interference ("*On dit* qu'on a vu même, en ce désordre affreux,/Un dieu ..." (1539-40; italics added), he ultimately acknowledges the triumph of "the gods' wrath" (1539). In turning to the plural Théramène echoes Thésée, who had first called on Neptune to avenge him (1157), was anguished at the "dieux impatients" (1496) before the report, and becomes resentful of the "inexorables dieux" (1572) once he is fully informed. Seneca's Theseus had assumed full responsibility for Hippolytus' tragic death (1208-11), which he had first ascribed to chance (1120), alluding only briefly to Neptune's "fatherly" readiness to grant his irate prayers (1207).[5] In Racine the emphasis rests on the wrath of the gods, their ironic cruelty and, through Hippolyte's dying words, the unfairness of a *ciel* that destroys his "innocent life" (1561). The shift from a single deity to "the gods" in general impresses on the reader the undifferentiated solidarity of arbitrary Omnipotence. The sacred is thus depicted as a triptych: Venus stands for the *deus absconditus*, God's refusal to award his saving grace to Phèdre and help her subdue her corrupt nature; the Sun and Minos jointly stand for *deus praesens*, the all-seing eye and supreme judge; while Neptune impersonates the perverse deceptiveness of an allegedly "tutelary" deity who is in fact a trickster god, who now reveals himself to be an accomplice of Venus in the victimizing of Phèdre as he grants Theseus' mistaken request in lethal irony, inflicting an appalling though undeserved death on poor Hippolyte.

We may legitimately speculate that Racine stuck to the unlikely mythicizing in the dramatic tradition because it suited his purpose to have the accidental intervention of some sea-beast engineered by a god. Renaissance dramatists might have linked it to "the stars" and the whims of "Fortune" which Augustine had argued are but manifestations incomprehensible to human reason of God's hidden designs.[6] In any modern view the death of Hippolyte as recounted by Théramène, once divested of all supernatural trappings, is just an unfortunate random coincidence occasioned by the vagaries of chance, the blind impersonal force that creates the situations with which man is confronted. In its deadly consequences it can indeed be compared to a tile falling from a roof on the head of an innocent passer-by.

Neptune thus belatedly reveals himself as a personalized projection of chance. As we look back from this vantage point, we are brought to realize the importance of the role played by chance in the preparation

---

[5] In describing Theseus as Neptune's son (*Phaed* 941-57), Seneca followed a recondite tradition reported by Apollodorus of Athens (180-*ca* 115 BC) in his *Bibliotheca*: "Journeying by way of Troezen [Aegeus] lodged with Pittheus ... who ... made him drunk and caused him to lie with his daughter Aethra. But in the same night Poseidon also had connexion with her" (3.15.7). Racine may have chosen to ignore this version because Plutarch claimed that Neptune's paternity was a fiction invented by Aethra (*Theseus* 6). It may also be that the malefic activity he attributed to the sea-god in *Phèdre* did not seem congruent with the majestic status of a father figure.

[6] Augustine's *De libero arbitrio* (III, 2), quoted in Delumeau, 173.

of Phèdre's tragedy. After all it was by no means inevitable that she should marry a man with such an attractive son as Hippolyte; nor was it inevitable that her husband should call her to Troezen just as she had already gone a long way towards mastering her passion. The convergence of a number of chance events created the dramatic situation in which her ego became a plaything between the warring segments of her unconscious self, her id and her super-ego, thus generating what Freud was later to call "the tension between the demands of conscience and the actual performances of the ego [which] is experienced as a sense of guilt" (XIX, 37).

CONCLUSION

In this our post-modern age it would be idle to ignore that the original Phaidra story was imagined and organized by the long-forgotten oral bard who initiated the tradition. His purpose, however, was not solely or even primarily of an aesthetic order. He used his verbal skill in order to convey an educational message, a fundamental religious, social and moral prohibition. It was in the same spirit that later writers for more than two millennia shaped and reshaped the story, probing the values and beliefs of their own society or challenging the assumptions of their own culture. The dread of incest, we know, inspired one of the most archaic and most enduring socio-ethical interdictions in human civilization. According to Claude Lévi-Strauss its appearance marked the very inception of human culture. So powerful is the taboo that until recently straight mother-son incest proved totally unacceptable for artistic treatment. The motif of the stepmother enamoured of her stepson was less objectionable if handled with due tact, even though it took second place in what is probably the earliest written formulation, Leviticus 19. This situation was even more striking and its handling more conclusive when the outraged party was not just an ordinary husband and father but a ruler as well: the threat to the stability of the family group and the violation of "natural" restraint were thus compounded with an infringement of the social hierarchy.

As a choice example of nearly inconceivable transgression, the Phaedra syndrome could not fail to stimulate writers' profound engagement with ethical questions related to the very essence of criminal behaviour as defined by their own cultures. As manipulated by Euripides, Seneca and Racine the Phaedra story and its analogues in Bandello's *novella* and Lope de Vega's *comedia* have proved liable to a number of readings. But beyond the artists' proper urge to produce good plays, their purpose has always been to analyse their characters' impulses, the motives underlying their resistance or acquiescence, the values justifying or invalidating their behaviour as such things could be appraised in the context of their culture. Close attention broadens our awareness of the specific identity of people quite unlike ourselves and deepens our sensitiveness to the historic course of culture change.

Euripides' *Hippolutos* conveys the playwright's dissatisfaction with ancient belief in pagan gods and with an honour code based on a person's image in public opinion; his Phaidra is a truly tragic figure, confused and misled by the ambiguities in the ethos of her times. In his yearning for some inner principle of morality, Euripides' contemporary Democritus would have found Seneca's play more gratifying. A thoroughly evil woman, the Latin Phaedra yields to her illicit desires depite her better knowledge. Her ultimate fate vindicates the Nurse's early insight and demonstrates that conscience based on reason rather than fear of public opinion is the final criterion of righteousness.

Since Euripides five centuries had elapsed when Seneca turned the story into an illustration of the workings of an inner sense, hypostatized as *ratio*, *pudor* or *conscientia*, uninfluenced by either physical threat or social appraisal. This was also the time when an obscure Jewish preacher known as Jesus launched a movement that was to reach unforeseeable proportions and durably curb the rationalistic tradition of Greco-Roman Stoicism in a new direction. At a very early stage in their recorded history the Jews had developed the highly original concept of a unique supreme being, a personal deity of purely spiritual nature, endowed, though to a suprahuman degree, with the human qualities of intellect and will, all-knowing and all-powerful. The Lord, whose name is too sacred for utterance, is both the source of moral commandments and the infallible administrator of strict justice. Judaism emphasized man's duty to obey the will of God: it is not man's business to probe the Lord's motives or to question his justice. That such a creed at times raised baffling problems of theodicy can be seen in the Book of Job. Such problems have no solution within the compass of human reasoning. Job finds wisdom and recovers the friendship of the Lord (together with his property) when he acknowledges that he had "uttered that I understood not; things too wonderful for me, which I knew not ... Wherefore I abhor myself, and repent in dust and ashes" (Job 42: 3, 6). This withdrawal from rationality clearly anticipates an important trend in Christian thought. Since God, by definition, is always right, the trials to which the faithful are submitted cannot but be in some way justified; the main task of man's understanding is to identify the sins for which he is rightly punished; hence the sense of guilt and the anxiety which permeated Jewish culture for many centuries. In the course of time, however, Judaic theology evolved the notion of divine mercy, which was to become prominent in the teaching of Jesus: man is free, he has the capacity to change his heart and his ways, and so obtain God's pardon. Nevertheless it is a fact, as Paul Johnson observed, that the Jews "were the first to introduce the concept of repentance and atonement, which became a primary Christian theme also" (159).

By spreading to Europe the Judaic idea of a supreme being that is pure spirit, Christianity gave ethical theory a dimension of spiritual transcendence which was unknown to the classical world. The distinction between right and wrong, good and evil, was no longer a matter of avoiding physical retribution or ensuring social approval or even of acting rationally: it was a matter of obeying God's commands. Such a momentous development in the evolution of religious and ethical thought could not but affect later authorial interpretations of the Phaedra story through which weighty moral themes had proved capable of playing themselves out.

Amid the confusing proliferation of doctrines that entered into heated controversy and competition in the fourth century, once the Christian religion had been officially recognized and the Church had become associated with imperial power, two trends are of central importance for the future of ethical thought. One stressed the benevolence of the deity and asserted the freedom of man's will, its power to deserve eternal salvation by its own unaided strength. This view was represented by Pelagius, a cleric from Britain, who believed in the innate capabilities of human nature and rejected the notion that the Original Sin entailed the universal corruption of mankind. The opposite view was represented by a bishop from North Africa, Augustine, who had been attracted to Manicheism before he converted to Christianity. He emphasized the absolute power of the godhead and the inherent corruption of man, leading to the depressing prospect that the vast majority of mankind are doomed to eternal torments in hell, from which will be spared only the happy few who are enabled to achieve holiness through God's arbitrary and parsimonious grace. Augustine's pathological hatred of sex derives from his notion of the hereditary transmission of Original Sin.

Though Augustine emerged victorious from the dispute and his ideas became the Roman Church's official doctrine, his pessimistic conception of predestination was obviously suitable only for a tiny élite of ascetic spirituals. In the course of the ensuing centuries the Church felt a pragmatic need to develop a variety of compromise measures fit for the average man: it forcefully proclaimed such unlikely oxymora as the conjunction of infinite justice and infinite mercy in the godhead or the compatibility of divine omnipotence with human freedom; it instituted the sacrament of confession; it invented Purgatory as a half-way place where sinful souls could be purged of evil and at length be admitted into Paradise; it offered "indulgences", often in exchange for money or real estate. Such gimmicks enabled ordinary weak humans to pursue their self-indulgent ways in the two main fields of instinctual life, sex and aggressiveness, while entertaining the hope of eschewing hell fire, if only through confession *in articulo mortis*. It is this compromise which Bandello implicitly advocated through Ugo d'Este's edifying death. Nevertheless, the punishment the young man is determined to shun remains an external sanction. He offers little evidence of genuine inwardness: he simply transfers the primal physical fear of bodily suffering, which he cannot escape, to the pseudo-metaphysical torments that had been so efficiently described in countless sermons and morality plays, in sculptures and frescoes throughout the Middle Ages.

Democritus would no doubt have been disappointed at the spiritual mediocrity of Bandello's male protagonist. The Italian writer's perfunctory account of Ugo's manner of preparing for death is all too obviously a thin veneer designed to placate such devout readers as might have been dismayed by the tale itself. The alterations to which the *novella* was subjected by later adapters and translators suggest that this was felt to be regrettably inadequate. To the religiously minded the fact that the young man after eating his terrestrial cake is still entitled to a celestial one could not but remain unpalatable, despite the more elaborate comments appended by Bandello's followers: such ritualistic appropriation of the holy sacrament of confession, though intended as a practical compromise, appeared rather as an unacceptable surrender of principle. It was as a rebellion against such a betrayal of what he regarded as the spiritual essence of Christianity that Luther felt impelled to provoke the great religious crisis of the sixteenth century.

While this crisis pitted Protestants against Catholics in often murderous controversy, it is more appropriate to observe that within each camp there emerged a significant division between the radical upholders of spiritual inwardness — Calvinists, Puritans, Pietists in Protestant Europe and later Jansenists in Catholic France — and those who chose to remain sensitive to the practical need of compromising between the requirements of human weakness and the demands of moral theology. The foremost representatives of the latter attitude in the Roman church were the Jesuits, who were responsible for a theory described as "probabilism" which was eminently convenient, as Henry Sullivan noted, "as a method for offering easy absolution, especially to potentates whom they wished to influence in their campaign to undermine secular government for the benefit of the Vatican, or else to ordinary people disconcerted by the sternness of religious commandments" (44).

Probabilist casuistry is enacted in many Spanish *comedias* to remarkable dramatic effect. The Duke of Ferrara's convoluted soliloquies at the end of *El castigo sin venganza* are designed to reassure him that God's will coincides with his murderous obligation under the honour code. The same syncretically oriented outlook applies to Federico and Casandra: their affair is as grievous a transgression of the social code as of religious morality and Lope makes more of the latter element than did Bandello. Both lovers are rightly punished on both counts, but one reason why the Spanish playwright altered the original ending and did not allow the young man time to recant is that he was determined to make his theological message quite explicit: God's grace is not delivered as a matter of course; faith alone does not guarantee salvation. The young pair's manner of death must be seen as a warning that death comes like a thief in the night; therefore men had better avoid misusing for evil ends the freedom God has given them. The same point is made in an even more sensational way in Tirso de Molina's *El burlador de Sevilla*. Once they have embarked on their sinful life, Lope's characters, like Bandello's, fail to display the inner anxiety that is associated with a genuine sense of guilt. Their awareness that they are infringing God's law is on a par with their short-lived concern for the honour of the Duke. Even after their affair has been discovered they do not show any sign of remorse, and they allow themselves to be carried away by lust and jealousy. Their disgraceful ultimate plottings are clearly designed to highlight their increasingly degraded passions, which are stronger than their fear of retribution. Punishments, whether physical on earth or "spiritual" in the other world, appear to them external sanctions inflicted by outside agencies.

El castigo sin venganza is a typical baroque drama, whose action develops according to the principle enunciated by A. Reichenberger, "from order disturbed to order restored". This, at any rate, is no doubt how contemporary audiences saw it: God's order is restored when the sinners are duly disposed of; and so is the social order since the wrong done to the Duke's honour is punished in compliance with the Spanish requirement for secrecy. The Duke's decision even enhances his moral stature, since he had to repress his fatherly love in order to comply with the obligations imposed by God and society. In this way Lope constructed an image of cosmic order in which private affections are heroically subordinated to the joint requirements of the higher instances: religion and society. The modern reader, however, who does not share baroque assumptions, is unlikely to miss the element of sophistry in the Duke's (and Lope's) casuistry: after all it owes its validity to the accidental circumstance that the wronged father and husband is also a head of state, and as such the legitimate vicar of God in his tiny dukedom. The play is a superb example of Jesuitic probabilism at work. We may doubt whether our hypothetical, long-lived Democritus would have felt satisfied.

The Counter-Reformation managed to restore dogmatic authority and church discipline in Catholic countries, but it did little to instil genuine inwardness among the mass of the faithful. The church-inspired contribution to the development of baroque art in the seventeenth century, whether in architecture, sculpture, painting or in drama, was of high aesthetic quality. It was also calculated to generate admiration and fear through its ostentatious, awe-inspiring display of power and opulence. Nevertheless, a genuine sense of internalized spirituality manifested itself in the teachings of the Catholic bishop of Ypres, then in the Spanish Low Countries, Cornelius Jansen (1585-1638), better known as Jansenius, whose posthumously published treatise, *Augustinus* (1640), provided a close equivalent to Calvin's radicalism: it reasserted Augustine's doctrine of predestination and grace and repudiated the efficacy of the human will. Jansenism soon incurred the hostility of the Jesuits, who upheld free will (controlled by confessors) and were afraid of losing their monopoly in education and spiritual direction. Its teachings were condemned by mainstream theologians in the Sorbonne. Several of its theses were censured by the Pope. Its adherents were persecuted by Louis XIV. Despite such opposition, Jansenius' rejction of scholasticism, formalism and casuistry appealed to a number of exacting minds who disseminated his ideas from the Cistercian convent of Port-Royal.

The most important writer associated with Jansenism is of course Pascal. But Racine had a close if volatile rapport to the *Messieurs de Port-Royal*, one of whose schools he attended for three years from the age of sixteen. He shared the Jansenists' concern with the deepening of religious life, but he was by no means immune to the allurements of worldly life. As a budding dramatist he broke for a while with Port-Royal in 1666 after one of its most learned theologians, Pierre Nicole, had issued a pamphlet branding novelists and playwrights as "empoisonneurs publics". Yet he could not accept what radical Christians regarded as "Jesuit laxity". As a bright, ambitious, sensual young man, whose yielding to worldly temptations, especially of a sexual order, dismayed his devout family, he could not but be affected by the torturing contradiction between the high moral demands of his creed and his actual sinful experience of the world. In his inability to resist such temptations, he had to face the central question raised by Augustine's doctrine of predestination: if God is all-powerful and his creatures ontologically powerless to resist evil, who is guilty? Racine's answer can be legitimately inferred from his characters' numberless blasphemous utterances blaming the cruelty and injustice of their ancient deities. *Phèdre* is the tragedy that made him fully conscious of the dangerous implications in the symbolic, vicarious discourse of his *oeuvre*. It was this, rather than the hostility of his envious rivals or the success of the cabal in favour of Pradon's mediocre *Phèdre et Hippolyte*, that prompted him to abandon classical subject-matter and to give up play-writing altogether for twelve years.

For the history of Western culture, however, the important point does not reside in the blasphemous statements in the play or in Racine's implicit recantation, but in the fact that the problem itself had been dramatized with such disturbing clarity. For this was characteristic of the times. I have quoted Pierre Bayle's abstract formulation in the first decade of the next century. But even in Racine's day this vital conundrum had been raised in quite explicit, though biased, terms by Blaise Pascal himself. As an exacting scientist and an outspoken critic of the facilities offered by Jesuitic probabilism, the author of the *Lettres provinciales* could not but acknowledge his intellectual dismay at doctrines such as Original Sin, which were admittedly repugnant to reason. But he phrased it in such a way as to deprecate reason and reaffirm the superiority of faith and unquestioning adherence to revelation and dogma. Here is part of item 434 in his *Pensées:*

> il est sans doute qu'il n'y a rien qui choque plus notre raison que de dire que le péché du premier homme ait rendu coupables ceux qui, étant si éloignés de cette source, semblent incapables d'y participer. Cet écoulement ne nous paraît pas seulement impossible, il nous semble même très injuste; car qu'y a-t-il de plus contraire aux règles de notre misérable justice que de damner éternellement un enfant incapable de volonté, pour un péché où il paraît avoir si peu de part, qu'il est commis six mille ans avant qu'il fût en être? Certainement rien ne nous heurte plus rudement que cette doctrine; et cependant, sans ce mystère, le plus incompréhensible de tous, nous sommes incompréhensibles à nous-mêmes. (185)

"Incomprehensible", "inexplicable", "contrary to reason and justice": such phrases recurred with increasing frequency in philosophical discourse as the seventeenth century was nearing its end: Descartes's "doute méthodique" — an epistemological prelude to the scientific quest for truth — was giving way to the anguish of metaphysical doubt as the spirit of free critical enquiry initiated by the Renaissance was making headway in Western minds. Like many of his contemporaries, Racine sought (and, one hopes, found) inner peace in blind submission to Faith and the teachings of the Church. But their awareness of (and occasional rebellion against) the irrationality and contradictions in the dogmatic statements of theology were a significant step, however negative and temporary, in the direction of Enlightenment rationalism, a necessary phase in the dechristianization of Europe. Meanwhile the ancient incest taboo had been endowed with a new, moral dimension: it was now branded as a mortal sin. What sets Racine's Phèdre apart from Bandello's and Lope's incestuous lovers is that despite her obdurate resistance to temptation and her vocal rebellion against the cruel power of the gods, she is beset by a deep sense of guilt: Democritus would have felt undiluted admiration even though he would have been dismayed at the psychoanalytical interpretation put forward in this book.

To discuss Racine's masterpiece in terms of Freudian psychology may be regarded as unforgivably anachronistic. Yet literary history shows that the Phaedra myth, the incest taboo and even the old cautionary tale have maintained much of their relevance, albeit in modified forms, throughout recent centuries. What I have in mind is not the many plays, poems and pieces of prose fiction that have been devoted to the Cretan queen since the days of Racine.[1] Nor is this the place to consider another analogon, the Don Carlos story, in which the private theme of incest became linked with the wider political theme of the uses and abuses of political power.[2] In fact the most ambitious and successful treatment of the Phaedra syndrome since Racine's is to be found in *La curée* (1871), Emile Zola's second novel in the Rougon-Macquart series. As Auguste Dezalay, a noted Zola scholar, discovered in 1971, it was in the course of writing this novel that Zola revealingly jotted down in a note-book: "Décidément, c'est une nouvelle Phèdre que je veux faire."

In the whole of his *oeuvre*, it was Zola's single-minded, wide-embracing purpose to offer a merciless portrayal and indictment of French society under Napoléon III. In *La Curée* his procedure was to associate, as he put it in his own Preface, "la note de l'or et de la chair". The theme of greed is impersonated in the career of the rags-to-riches tycoon, Aristide Saccard, while sexual debasement is illustrated in the affair between his promiscuous wife, Renée, and his effeminate son, Maxime. The similarity with the basic Phaedra situation was hinted at by Zola himself when he has Renée and Maxime attend a performance of Racine's tragedy. In recent years several critics have enlarged on the parallels to be found in character delineation and plot development.[3] But the divergences in outlook are even more revealing. Not without reason did Sandy Petrey dub *La Curée* "an anti-*Phèdre*" in which "a lascivious Hippolytus, an ignoble Theseus and an eager Phaedra stage a farce whose conclusion is a real estate transaction" (636). Zola was concerned with showing how the general corruption of Second Empire society is embodied in the private corruption of its individual members. It is a measure of his genius that he availed himself of Taine's theory on the influence of the environment to create an organic causal link between the two spheres of greed and sex: in a letter of 6 November 1871 he described the unpleasant liaison as "l'inceste grandi dans le

---

[1] For a historical introduction, see Amodeo's Italian essay of 1930.

[2] The Don Carlos theme, which has been discussed by Frederick Leiner, is best illustrated in Schiller's tragedy; it focuses on the son of King Philip II of Spain, who was allegedly in love with his father's second wife, Elisabeth de Valois.

[3] For in-depth descussions after Dezalay, see the essays by Sandy Petrey, Sara Via, Clayton Alcorn and Brian Nelson, listed in the Bibliography.

terreau des millions".[4] Renée Saccard's moral degradation is conditioned by the deleterious nouveau-riche milieu to which her marriage has given her access. In the luxurious boredom of her idleness she is unable to withstand her yearning for ever more refined, ultimately criminal, sensations.

This should not be taken to mean that Renée is just a lewd woman as we may presume Euripides' first Phaidra and Potiphar's wife to have been. She does have scruples, however ineffectual. She is aware of the criminal nature of her lust. She is endowed with rudimentary moral impulses which are constantly linked to her memories of innocent childhood pleasures and of her father. This retired magistrate, who hardly intervenes in person in the action, is clearly a Minos-like figure, as remote as in Racine, and a symbol for the stern integrity of a social class whose values have now vanished. The only positive character in the cast, Renée's father is explicitly described as the origin of her conscience and of the sense of shame that torments her at times: "elle appartenait à son père, à cette race calme et prudente où fleurissent les vertus du foyer" (421). One cannot help recalling the conjunction of Minos and the Sun in the shaping of Phèdre's super-ego, the Christian conception of God as the source of moral precepts, or, for that matter, Freud's statement in *Totem und Tabu*:

> The psycho-analysis of individual human beings ... teaches us with quite special insistence that the god of each of them is formed in the likeness of his father, that his personal relation to God depends upon his relation to his father in the flesh ... and that at bottom God is nothing other than an exalted father (XIII, 149).

La Curée is of course a secular novel, without any theological or metaphysical implications: Renée's behaviour is totally under the influence of her milieu, which encourages her to gratify her instincts and easily cancels whatever action the example and teachings of her father may ever have had upon her. This may seem surprising in view of Zola's well-known theories on the impact of heredity. Even more surprising in this respect is the fact that Renée's mother is barely mentioned in the novel: she is said to have died when her daughter was a mere child. Nevertheless, while watching *Phèdre*, the young woman is impressed by the similarity, and wonders: "Phèdre était du sang de

---

[4] The letter has been printed in vol. XIV of Henri Mitterand's edition of Zola's *Oeuvres complètes* (see 1375). Quotations from *La Curée* refer to Armand Lanoux's Pléiade edition of *Les Rougon-Macquart*.

Pasiphaé, et [Renée] se demandait de quel sang elle pouvait être, elle, l'incestueuse des temps nouveaux" (508). This is a question which Zola was to answer ten years later in *Renée*, the dramatic adaptation of the novel that he wrote at Sarah Bernhardt's request. Here at last we are apprised that Renée's mother belonged to a tainted family and had eloped with her husband's secretary. It was this added information which allowed Zola to claim, in his Preface to the play, "j'ai détruit le symbole de la fatalité antique, en mettant scientifiquement Renée sous la double influence de l'hérédité et des milieux" (ix) — a remarkable flash of insight into the evolution of the Phaedra syndrome.

Zola's claim to "scientific" validity was of course exceedingly naive, deluded as he was by the then fashionable ideology of Positivism. The point, however, is that the violation of the incest taboo was now treated with utmost explicitness and in overtly biological and psychological terms. It is true that, although the novelist never uses such terms of ethical judgement as "evil" or "sin", Renée's story was conceived as a forceful condemnation of the way an individual's private life might be wrecked by the corruption of French Second Empire society. This, however, was not how it was received. The novel shocked many readers and critics. Their attitude is reflected in a letter from the then director of the Comédie Française, which Zola quoted on his Preface to *Renée*, containing a frank warning that "le public ne supporterait pas la Phèdre moderne possédée par son fils, presque sous les yeux de son époux" (iii).

It was unavoidable that the artistic handling of the Phaedra syndrome and, more generally, of the incest taboo, should be profoundly affected by the dialectics of rapid culture change in the twentieth century. The early decades were the time when champions of public morality strove to impose their austere standards: the works of James Joyce, D.H. Lawrence and Henry Miller were banned in English-speaking countries and William Hays, post-master general in President Harding's administration, was entrusted with the task of deciding what is acceptable in the new mass medium, film, in all matters concerning religion, crime and sex. Aimed at improving the world, such censorship proved powerless to check the evolution of public taste. As Harold Laski observed many years ago, by 1930 the number of Hollywood movies dealing with sex and violence represented "an important increase over the figures of 1920" (683).

One of the most pregnant features in modern age culture is that the scientific approach — which nineteenth-century Positivism and Zola's naturalism had clumsily anticipated — succeeded in eliminating all vestiges of the traditional ethical premises derived from theological assumptions. More specifically, Freud's research into the erstwhile unfathomed depths of the individual psyche inaugurated an unprejudiced secular attitude to sex and sexual activities among psychology scholars. The generalization of literacy in Western society, the rapid growth of the new mass media and the efficacy of modern contraception techniques are only a few of the factors that coalesced to spawn postwar permissive society, one of whose most conspicuous characteristics is the liberation of sex from ethical considerations. When the Phaedra syndrome resurfaced in any significant way, it was on the silver screen, with Ingmar Bergman's international success, *Smiles of a Summer Night* (1956). In this, for the austere Swedish cineast untypical comedy, the incestuous elopment of stepmother and stepson is a mere sub-plot in a fairly complex story whose main interest is as a satirical commentary on modern marriage. Bergman's humorous treatment implies no moral outrage, no condemnation however discreet: on the contrary, the ending hails the healthy triumph of youthful natural instincts over the hypocritical conventions of the adult world.

The trivialization of sex in art did not stop there. In the seventies, a more daringly innovative generation of film-makers, finding the stepmother a cumbersome, perhaps hypocritical, device, managed to do away with this central figure in the Phaedra syndrome. In *Le Souffle au coeur* (1971) Louis Malle inserted a tenderly erotic lovemaking scene between mother and son, which failed to raise the expected outcry. At the end, the incestuous mother protectively undertakes, with complete success, to prevent the emergence of guilt feelings in the delicate mind of her adolescent son: the incident, she explains in terms that seem to parody Thésée's *Verneinung* in Racine, has been but a pleasant isolated episode, which had better be forgotten and never mentioned again. And in 1979 Bernardo Bertolucci's *La Luna* cheerfully violated what had been for countless centuries the object of the ultimate taboo, direct mother-son incest: it is now awarded therapeutic efficacy when the mother in the film, a famous *diva*, proceeds to the sexual initiation of her son in the hope of curing a neurosis induced by parental absenteeism.

Such developments will certainly supply observers of our *fin-de-siècle* society, its mores and ethical premises with abundant food for thought. They seem to indicate that the diffusion of popular psychoanalysis paradoxically excludes sexual activities in any form whatsoever from the jurisdiction of the super-ego as originally defined by Sigmund Freud. A minor consequence may well be that the Phaedra syndrome in its "pure" form and whoever its protagonists may be will cease to be regarded as a relevant topic for serious aesthetic treatment.

A literary scholar may nevertheless be pardoned for doubting whether such major achievements as those of Euripides, Seneca, Lope de Vega, Racine and Zola will ever lose their vibrancy, their ability to command attendance and attention from future generations of audiences and critics. For such works are inherently polysemic: this is the key to their durability. They inevitably reflect the culture, assumptions and problems of their authors' times, but they can be interpreted anew and still make sense even when the course of history has deeply altered the outlook of society. I have tried to show that Racine's *Phèdre* has been legitimately understood in a variety of ways, not least plausibly through the psychoanalytical approach that was evolved in the twentieth century. But while this tragedy, like most of the other works that have been discussed in this book, is a historically produced artefact largely shaped by time-bound circumstances identifiable in terms of both the cultural context and the writer's personal experience, the same is true of any interpretation that can be elaborated by individual analysts at any given time. Some future scholar may find it more adequate to explicate Racine's masterpiece in terms of chromosomes, genes and hormones, of "sexual selection", "female choice" and "male competition". On the other hand, it is not inconceivable that Western culture, in its revulsion against the crude materialism generated by the electronic revolution, the revolting social aftermath of so-called "liberalism" and the hedonistic laxity derived from sexual liberation, may seek comfort in new forms of spiritual idealism. The growth of fundamentalism and integrism in established religions and the proliferation of esoteric sects may herald a more general return to irrationality. This might entail a reappraisal of *Phèdre* in the light of concepts redolent of the radical outlook of the late seventeenth century.

Whether either of these trends will represent loss or enrichment is for the next century to discover.

BIBLIOGRAPHY

Alonso Amado, "Lope de Vega y sus fuentes", *Thesaurus* (Colombia), 8 (1952), 1-24.
Alcorn, Clayton, "*La Curée*: Les deux Renée Saccard", *Cahiers naturalistes*, 51 (1977), 49-55.
Alter, Robert, *The Pleasures of Reading*, New York, 1989.
Amodeo, E., *Da Euripide a d'Annunzio: Fedra e Ippolito nella tragedia classica e nella moderna*, Rome, 1930.
Apollodorus of Athens, *The Library*, trans. James Frazer, Loeb Classical Library, 1989.
Bandello, Matteo, *Tutte le opere de Matteo Bandello*, ed. Francesca Flora, Milan, 1934.
Barko, Ivan P., "La Symbolique de Racine: Essai d'interpretation des images de lumière et de ténèbres dans la vision tragique de Racine", *Revue des Sciences Humaines*, 115 (1964), 353-57.
Barnes, Hazel E., "The Hippolytus of Drama and Myth" in *Hippolytus in Drama and Myth*, Lincoln: Nebraska, 1960, 69-123.
Barrault, Jean-Louis, *"Phèdre" de Jean Racine*, Paris, 1946.
Barthes, Roland, *Sur Racine*, Paris, 1963.
Bénichou, Paul, *Morales du grand siècle*, Paris, 1948.
-----, *L'Ecrivain et ses travaux*, Paris, 1948.
Bodson, Arthur, "Sénèque et le suicide", in *Actas del Congreso Internacional de Filosofia*, Madrid, 1966, 91-107.
Bossuet, Jacques Bénigne, *Traité de la concupiscence*, ed. F. Levesque, Paris, 1920.
Bowra, C.M., "The Simplicity of Racine", in Knight, *Racine*, London 1969, 24-48.
Boyle, Anthony James, "In Nature's Bond: A Study of Seneca's *Phaedra*", in *Aufstieg und Niedergang der römischen Welt*, II. 32.2, 1284-1347.
Bremer, J.M., S.L. Radt and C.J. Ruijgh, eds, *Miscellanea tragica in honorem J.C. Kamerbeek*, Amsterdam, 1976.
Butler, Philip, *Classicisme et baroque dans l'oeuvre de Racine*, Paris, 1959.
-----, *Racine: A Study*, London, 1974.
Butor, Michel, "Racine et les dieux", *Lettres nouvelles*, 10 June 1959, 10 (reprinted in *Répertoire*, Paris, 1960, 28-60).
Cairncross, John, trans., *Racine: Iphigenia, Phaedra, Athaliah*, Penguin, 1972.
Castiglione, Baldassare, *Il libro del cortegiano*, ed. Bruno Maier, Turin, 2nd edn, 1964.
Claus, D., "Phaedra and the Socratic Paradox", *Yale Classical Studies*, 22 (1972), 223-38.
Coleridge, Samuel Taylor, *Lay Sermons*, ed. R.J. White, *Collected Works of Samuel Taylor Coleridge*, VI, London, 1972.
Correa, Gustavo, "El doble aspecto de la honra en el teatro del siglo XVII", *Hispanic Review*, 26 (1958), 99-107.
Council, Norman, *When Honour's at the Stake: Ideas of Honour in Shakespeare's Plays*, London, 1973.
Craik, Elizabeth M., "Euripides' First *Hippolytos*", *Mnemosyne*, 40 (1987), 137-39.

Criado del Val, Manuel, ed., *Lope de Vega y las origenes del teatro español*, Madrid, 1981.
Croisille, J.M., "Lieux communs, *sententiae* et intentions philosophiques dans la *Phèdre* de Sénèque", *Revue des Etudes Latines*, 42 (1964), 271-301.
Dam, C.F. Adolfo van, ed., *Lope de Vega: El castigo sin venganza*, Groningen, 1928.
Davis, Peter J., "*Vindicat Omnes Natura Sibi*: A Reading of Seneca's *Phaedra*", *Ramus*, 3 (1983), 114-27.
Delcroix, Maurice, *Le Sacré dans les tragédies profanes de Racine: Essai sur la signification du dieu mythologique dans "La Thébaïde", "Iphigénie" et "Phèdre"*, Paris, 1970.
Delmas, Christian, "La mythologie dans la *Phèdre* de Racine", *Revue d'Histoire du Théâtre*, 23 (1971), 50-77.
Delumeau, Jean, *Le Péché et la peur: La culpabilisation en Occident (XIIIe-XVIIIe siècles)*, Paris, 1983.
Deroux, Carl, ed., *Studies in Latin Literature and Roman History*, III, Brussels, 1983.
Dezalay, Auguste, "La 'nouvelle Phèdre' de Zola ou Les mésaventures d'un personnage tragique", *Travaux de Linguistique et de Littérature* (Strasbourg), 9, ii (1971), 121-34.
Dingel, Joachim, "Ἱππόλυτος Ξιφουλκος. Zu Senecas *Phaedra* und dem ersten *Hippolytos* des Euripides", *Hermes*, 98 (1970), 44-56.
Diodorus Siculus, *The Library of History*, ed. and trans. C.H. Oldfather, Loeb Classical Library, 1952.
Dixon, Victor, "*El castigo sin venganza*: The Artistry of Lope de Vega", in R.O. Jones, 63-81.
----- and A.A. Parker, "*El castigo sin venganza*: Two lines, two interpretations", *Modern Language Notes*, 85 (1970), 430-35.
Dodds, E.R., "The ΑΙΔΩΣ of Phaedra and the Meaning of *Hippolytus*", *Classical Review*, (1925), 102-104.
-----, *The Greeks and the Irrational*, Berkeley, 1951.
Dubu, Jean, "De quelques raisons esthétiques du silence de Racine après *Phèdre*", *XVIIe Siècle*, 20 (1953), 341-49. Eng. trans. in Knight, *Racine*, 218-30.
Eigeldinger, Marc, *La Mythologie solaire dans l'oeuvre de Racine*, Geneva, 1969.
Erffa, Carl Eduard von, *Aidôs und verwandte Begriffe in ihrer Entwicklung von Homer bis Demokrit*, in *Philologus*, Supplementblatt 30 (1937).
Die Fragmente der Vorsokratiker, ed. Hermann Diels, Berlin, 1966-67.
Frenzel, Elisabeth, *Stoffe der Weltliteratur*, 2nd edn, Stuttgart, 1963.
-----, *Motive der Weltliteratur*, Stuttgart, 1980.
Freud, Sigmund, *The Standard Edition of the Complete Psychological Works*, trans. and ed. James Strachey, in collaboration with Anna Freud, assisted by Alix Strachey and Alan Tyson, 24 vols, London, 1953-74.
García Valdecasas, Alfonso, *El hidalgo y el honor*, Madrid, 1948.
Gibbon, Edward, "Antiquities of the House of Brunswick", in *Miscellaneous Works*, London, 1796.
Gide, André, *Attendu que ...*, Paris, 1943.
Gigas, Emile, "Etudes sur quelques *comedias* de Lope de Vega", *Revue Hispanique*, 53 (1921), 589-604.
Giomini, Remo, *Saggi sulla "Fedra" di Seneca*, Rome, 1955.
Goldmann, Lucien, *Le Dieu caché: Etudes sur la vision tragique dans les "Pensées" de Pascal et dans le théâtre de Racine*, Paris, 1956.

Gould, J., "HIKETEIA", *Journal of Hellenic Studies*, 93 (1973), 74-104.
Graves, Robert, *Greek Myths*, 4th edn, London, 1965.
Green, Otis H., *Spain and the Western Tradition: The Castilian Mind from "El Cid" to Calderón*, Madison: Wisconsin, 4 vols, 1968.
Grene, David, "Introduction" to *Hippolytus*, in Grene and Lattimore, II, 158-60.
----- and Richmond Lattimore, eds, *The Complete Greek Tragedies: Euripides*, Chicago, 3 vols, n.d.
Grimal, Pierre, "L'originalité de Sénèque dans la tragédie de *Phèdre*", *Revue des Etudes Latines*, 41 (1963), 297-314.
-----, ed., *Sénèque, "Phaedra"*, Paris, 1965.
Hauvette, Henri, *L'Arioste et la poésie chevaleresque à Ferrare au début du XVIe siècle*, Paris, 1927.
Heldmann, Konrad, "Senecas *Phaedra* und ihre griechischen Vorbilder", *Hermes*, 96 (1968) 88-117.
-----, *Untersuchungen zu den Tragödien Senecas*, in *Hermes Einzelschriften*, 31, Zurich and Stuttgart, 1974.
Henry, Denis and B. Walker, "Phantasmagoria and Idyll: An Element of Seneca's *Phaedra*", *Greece and Rome*, 13 (1966), 223-39.
Herrmann, Léon, ed., *Le Théâtre de Sénèque*, Paris, 1924.
Herter, H., "Phaidra in griechischer und römischer Gestalt", *Rheinisches Museum*, 114 (1971), 44-77.
Hilborn, Henry W., "El creciente gongorismo en las comedias de Lope de Vega", in Kossoff and Amor y Vásquez, 281-94.
Homer, *The Odyssey*, Loeb Classical Library, 1953.
Hook, Frank, ed., *The French Bandello*, Columbia: Missouri, 1948.
Hubert, J.D., *Les Secrets témoins: Essai d'exégèse racinienne*, Paris, 1956.
Huizinga, Johan, *Le Déclin du Moyen Age*, Paris, 1932.
Issacharoff, Dora, "El origen histórico-literario de *El castigo sin venganza*: Resolución barroca de un conflicto manierista", in Criado del Val, 145-50.
Johnson, Paul, *A History of the Jews*, New York, 1987.
Jones, George Fenwick, *Honor in German Literature*, Chapel Hill, 1959.
Jones, R.O., ed., *Studies in Spanish Literature of the Golden Age Presented to Edward M. Wilson*, London, 1973.
Kaisergruber, Danielle, David Kaisergruber and Jacques Lempert, *"Phèdre" de Racine: Pour une sémiotique de la représentation classique*, Paris, 1972.
Kawashima, Shigenari, "ΑΙΔΩΣ and ΕΥΚΔΕΙΑ: Another Interpretation of Phaedra's Long Speech in the *Hippolytus*", *Studi Italiani di Filologia Classica*, 4 (1986), 183-94.
Keats, John, *The Letters of John Keats*, ed. M. Buxton Forman, London, 1945.
Kennedy, R.L., "The Theme of Stratonice in the Drama of the Spanish Peninsula", *PMLA*, 4 (1940), 1010-32.
Kitto, H.D.F., *Greek Tragedy* (1939), Anchor rpt, 1954.
Klein, Julius Leopold, *Geschichte des Dramas*, X, Leipzig, 1874.
Knight, R.C., *Racine et la Grèce*, Paris, 1952.
-----, ed., *Racine*, London, 1969.
Kossoff, A. David, *Lope de Vega: El perro del hortelano. El castigo sin venganza*, Madrid, 1970.

----- and José Amor y Vásquez, eds, *Homenaje a William L. Fichter: Estudios sobre el teatro antiquo hispánico y otros ensaios*, Madrid, 1971.
Kovacs, David, "Shame, Pleasure and Honor in Phaedra's Great Speech: Euripides, *Hippolytus* 375-87", *American Journal of Philology*, 101 (1980), 287-303.
Krailsheimer, A.J., *Studies in Self-Interest: From Descartes to La Bruyère*, Oxford, 1962.
Lanson, Gustave, *Histoire de la littérature française*, Paris, 1963.
Larson, Donald R., *The Honor Plays of Lope de Vega*, Cambridge: Mass., 1977.
Leeman, A.D., "Seneca's *Phaedra* as a Stoic Tragedy", in Bremer, 199-212.
Lefèvre, Eckard, "Quid ratio possit? Senecas *Phaedra* als stoisches Drama", *Wiener Studien*, 82 (1969), 131-60.
-----, ed., *Senecas Tragödien*, Darmstadt, 1972.
-----, ed., *Der Einfluß Senecas auf das europäische Drama*, Darmstadt, 1978.
Leiner, Frederick C., *The Don Carlos Theme*, Cambridge: Mass., 1930.
Lemaître, Jules, *Jean Racine*, Paris, 1908.
Lesky, Albin, *A History of Greek Literature*, trans. J. Willis and C. de Heer, 2nd edn, New York, 1963.
Levin, Donald Norman, "Phèdre and Oenone", *Rice University Studies*, 51/iii (1965), 51-68.
Livy, [*Works*], I, ed. B.O. Foster, Loeb Classical Library, 1919.
McCrary, William C., "The Duke and the *Comedia*: Drama and Imitation in Lope's *El castigo sin venganza*", *Journal of Hispanic Philology*, 2 (1978), 203-22.
MacDonald, I.I., "Why Lope?", *Bulletin of Spanish Studies*, 12 (1935), 185-97.
McKendrick, Malveena, *Woman and Society in the Spanish Drama of the Golden Age: A Study of the "mujer varonil"*, London, 1974.
Manuwald, Bernd, "Phaidras tragisches Irrtum: Zur Rede Phaidras in Euripides' *Hippolytos* (vv. 373-430)", *Rheinisches Museum*, 122 (1979), 134-48.
Maravall, José Antonio, *Culture of the Baroque*, trans. Terry Cochran, Manchester, 1986.
Maulnier, Thierry, *Lecture de "Phèdre"*, Paris, 1967.
Mauron, Charles, *L'Inconscient dans l'oeuvre de Racine*, Gap (France), 1957.
-----, *Phèdre*, Paris, 1968.
May, T.E., "Lope de Vega's *El castigo sin venganza*: The Idolatry of the Duke of Ferrara", *Bulletin of Hispanic Studies*, 37 (1960), 154-82.
Mead, Margaret, ed., *Cooperation and Competition Among Primitive Peoples*, New York, 1937.
Meier, Harri, *Ensaios de filologia românica*, Lisbon, 1948.
Menéndez Pidal, Ramón, *El P. Las Casas y Victoria con otros temas de los siglos XVI y XVII* (1958), Madrid, 1966.
Merzlack, Regina Fucito, "*Furor* in Seneca's *Phaedra*", in Deroux, 193-210.
Moline, J., "Euripides, Socrates, Virtue", *Hermes*, 103 (1975), 45-67.
Montesquieu, Charles Louis de, *Oeuvres*, ed. R. Caillois, Paris, 2 vols, 1955-58.
Nelson, Brian, "Speculation and Dissipation: A Reading of Zola's *La Curée*", *Essays in French Literature*, 14 (1977), 1-33.
Newton, Winifred, *Le Thème de Phèdre et d'Hippolyte dans la littérature française*, Paris, 1939.
Nichols, Geraldine, "The Rehabilitation of the Duke of Ferrara", *Journal of Hispanic Philology*, 1 (1977), 209-30.

Nixon, Victor, "The Symbolism of *Peribañez*", *Bulletin of Hispanic Studies*, 45 (1966), 11-24.
Noyes Jr., Russel, "Seneca on Death", *Journal of Religion and Health*, 12 (1973), 223-40.
Olechowska, Elżbieta, "Les Échos liviens dans la *Phèdre* de Sénèque", *Eos*, 67 (1979), 321-22.
Ong, Walter J., *Orality and Literacy: The Technologizing of the Word*, London, 1982.
Orlando, Francesco, *Toward a Freudian Theory of Literature, with an Analysis of Racine's "Phèdre"*, trans. Charmaine Lee, Baltimore, 1978.
Paratore, Ettore, "Sulla *Phaedra* di Seneca", *Dionisio* N.S., 15 (1952), 199-234.
-----, "Lo Ἱππόλυτος καλυπτόμενος di Euripide e la *Phaedra* di Seneca", in *Studi classici ... Catandella*, I, 303-46.
Parker, A.A., *The Approach to the Spanish Drama of the Golden Age*, London, 1957.
Pascal, Blaise, *Pensées*, ed., Ch.-M. Des Granges, Paris, 1958.
Peristiany, J.G., ed., *Honour and Shame: The Values of Mediterranean Society*, London, 1965.
Petrey, Sandy, "Stylistics and Society in *La Curée*", *Modern Language Notes*, 89 (1974), 626-40.
Picard, Raymond, ed., *Racine: Oeuvres complètes*, Paris, 1951.
-----, *De Racine au Parthénon: Essais sur la littérature et l'art de l'âge classique*, Paris, 1977.
Piers, Gerhart and Milton B. Singer, *Shame and Guilt*, Springfield: Ill., 1953.
Pitt-Rivers, Julian, "Honour and Social Status", in Peristiany, 19-67.
Plumb, J.H., *The Italian Renaissance* (1961), New York, 1965.
Plutarch, *Lives*, trans. Bernadette Perrin, Loeb Classical Library, 1920.
Pocock, Gordon, *Corneille and Racine: Problems of Tragic Form*, Cambridge, 1973.
Poetscher, Walter, "Nosse peccandi modum: Seneca, *Phaedra*, 141", *Emerita*, 44 (1976), 159-61.
Pohlenz, Max, *Die Stoa: Geschichte einer geistigen Bewegung*, ed. H. Doerrie, 3rd edn, Göttingen, 2 vols, 1964.
Pommier, Jean, *Aspects de Jean Racine*, Paris, 1954.
Poulet, Georges, *Etudes sur le temps humain*, Paris, 1950.
Pratt, Norman, "Two Types of Classical Tragedy: The Senecan Revolution", in Stallknecht and Frenz, 218-47.
Pring-Mill, R.D.F., "Introduction" to *Lope de Vega: Five Plays*, trans. Jill Booty, New York, 1961.
Regenbogen, Otto, *Kleine Schriften*, Munich, 1961.
Reichenberger, Arnold G., "The Uniqueness of the *Comedia*", *Hispanic Review*, 27 (1959), 303-16.
Reynier, Gustave, *Le Roman sentimental avant "L'Astrée*, Paris, 1908.
Rivier, André, "Discussion", in *Entretiens sur l'Antiquité classique*, 6 (1960), 196.
Romilly, Jacqueline de, "L'Excuse de l'invincible amour dans la tragédie grecque", in Bremer, 308-12.
Rymer, Thomas, *Tragedies of the Last Age*, London, 1978.
Schaeffer, Adolf, *Geschichte des spanischen Nationaldramas*, Leipzig, 1890.
Segal, Charles, "Shame and Purity in Euripides' *Hippolytus*", *Hermes*, 98 (1970), 278-99.
-----, *Language and Desire in Seneca's "Phaedra"*, Princeton, 1986.
Seidensticker, B., *Die Gesprächsverdichtung in den Tragödien Senecas*, Munich, 1961.

Seneca, *Moral Essays*, trans. J.W. Basore, Loeb Classical Library, 1951.
-----, *Ad Lucilium epistolae morales*, trans. R.M. Cummere, Loeb Classical Library, 1953.
Singer, Milton, "Shame Cultures and Guilt Cultures", in Piers and Singer, 45-86.
Snell, Bruno, "Das frühste Zeugnis über Sokrates", *Philologus*, 97 (1948), 125-34.
-----, *Scenes from Greek Drama*, Berkeley, 1967.
Solmsen, F., "Bad Shame and Related Problems in Phaidra's Speech", *Hermes*, 101 (1973), 420-25.
Spitzer, Leo, *Linguistics and Literary History*, Princeton, 1948.
Stallknecht, Newton P. and Horst Frenz, eds, *Comparative Literature: Methods and Perspectives*, Carbondale, 1961 (rev. edn Arcturus, 1973).
Starobinski, Jean, *L'Oeil vivant*, Paris, 1968.
Stone Jr., Donald, "Belleforest's Bandello: A Bibliographical Study", *Bibliothèque d'Humanisme et de Renaissance*, 34 (1972), 489-99.
-----, *From Tales to Truth: Essays on French Fiction in the Sixteenth Century*, Frankfurt, 1973 (*Analecta Romanica* 34).
Strabo, *Geography*, trans. H.L. Jones, Loeb Classical Library, 1928.
Strohm, Hans, *Euripides: Interpretationen zur dramatischen Form*, Munich, 1957.
Studi classici in onore di Quintino Catandella, Catania, 3 vols, 1972.
Sturel, René, *Bandello en France au XVIe siècle*, Bordeaux, 1918.
Suetonius II, trans. J.C. Rolfe, Loeb Classical Library, 1950.
Sullivan, Henry W., *Tirso de Molina and the Drama of the Counter Reformation*, Amsterdam, 1981.
Taplin, O. *Greek Tragedy in Action*, London, 1978.
Thomann, Theodor, ed., *Seneca: Sämtliche Tragödien*, Zurich and Stuttgart, 1961-69.
Toldo, Pietro, *Contributo allo studio della novella francese del XV e XVI seculo*, Rome, 1895.
Tortel, *Le Préclassicisme français*, Paris, 1952.
Triwedi, Mitchell, D., "The Source and Meaning of the Pelican Fable in *El castigo sin venganza*", *Modern Language Notes*, 92 (1977), 326-29.
Turato, F., "Seduzione della parola e dramma dei segni nell' *Ippolito* di Euripide", *Boletino dell'Istituto di Filologia greca dell'Università di Padova*, 3 (1976), 159-83.
Turnell, Martin, *The Classical Moment*, London, 1947.
-----, *Jean Racine, Dramatist*, London, 1972.
Valbuena-Briones, Angel, "El simbolismo en el teatro de Calderón: La caída de caballo", *Romanische Forschungen*, 74 (1962), 60-99.
Valbuena Pratt, A., *Historia de la literatura española*, Barcelona, 1960 (6th edn of vol. II).
Vega Carpio, Lope de, *Obras escogidas: I Teatro*, ed. F.C. Saínz de Robles, Madrid, 1952.
Venesoen, Constant, *Jean Racine et le procès de la culpabilité*, Paris, 1981.
Voltaire, *Oeuvres complètes*, XXXIV, Paris, 1818.
Vossler, Karl, *Jean Racine*, Munich, 1926.
-----, *Lope de Vega und sein Zeitalter*, Munich, 1932.
Vretska, H., "Zwei Interpretationsprobleme in Senecas *Phaedra*", *Wiener Studien* N.S., 2 (1968), 153-70.
Wagner, Christian, "Vernunft und Tugend in Euripides' Hippolytos", *Wiener Studien* N.S., 18 (1984), 37-51.

Watling, E.F., trans., *Seneca: Four Tragedies and "Octavia"*, Penguin, 1966.
Weinberg, Bernard, *The Art of Jean Racine*, Chicago, 1963.
White, Julian E., "Phèdre Is not Incestuous", *Romance Notes*, 9 (1967), 89-94.
Wilson E.M., "La Discreción de Don Lope de Almeida", *Clavileño*, 2/xix (1951), 1-10.
----- and Duncan Moir, *A Literary History of Spain. The Golden Age: Drama (1492-1700)*, London, 1971.
Winnington-Ingram, R.P., "*Hippolytus*: A Study in Causation", *Entretiens sur l'Antiquité classique*, 6 (1960), 169-91.
Zintzen, Cl., *Analytisches Hypomnena zu Senecas "Phaedra", Beiträge zur klassischen Philologie*, 1 (1960).
Zola, Emile, *Les Rougon-Macquart*, ed. Armand Lanoux, Paris, 1960.
-----, *Oeuvres complètes*, ed. Henri Mitterand, Paris, 1966-70.
-----, "Renée" in *Théâtre II*, ed. Maurice Le Blond, Paris, 1927.